# PASSIVE INCOME, AGGRESSIVE RETIREMENT

The Secret to Freedom, Flexibility, and
Financial Independence

(& how to get started!)

# DOWNLOAD YOUR FREE BONUS GIFT!

**READ THIS FIRST**

As a thank you for buying my book, I'm giving you a bonus gift of supplemental information about how to start building passive income, 100% FREE!

Your free bonus gift comes with the following:

- The top three deadly mistakes to avoid when creating your passive income stream
- A simple, customizable worksheet to determine which passive income stream you should pursue first
- A time tracker activity to motivate you to get started

And much more!

**TO DOWNLOAD GO TO:**

## www.moneyhoneyrachel.com/bonus

Follow me on social media!

Facebook: www.facebook.com/moneyhoneyrachel
Instagram: www.instagram.com/moneyhoneyrachel
Twitter: www.twitter.com/moneyhoneyrach

# TABLE OF CONTENTS

# INTRODUCTION

Let's be honest: At one point or another, we have *all* fantasized about being so filthy rich that our only concern is which cocktail to drink next as we enjoy the view from our beachfront home in California (or ski chalet in Vermont... or Tuscan villa in Italy... whatever makes ya hot). I can almost feel the warm sand beneath my toes, taste the red sangria, and hear the ocean waves breaking gently before me. Ahhh, the retired life, amirite?

Imagine a world that makes no demands of you. You don't have to worry about money. You don't have to be physically present in any particular place. You can hop on a plane tomorrow and go to Costa Rica if that's what your heart desires. You can spend your time on the things that fulfill you: painting, writing, volunteering, raising your kids, traveling. You don't have to *work*.

You're in luck because I have found—stumbled upon, really—a way to achieve financial independence and early retirement that has not yet been fully explored.

Sure, sure, there are a million books about retiring early and how to do it; in fact, there's an entire movement dedicated to this exact topic: Financial Independence Retire Early (FIRE). The FIRE movement has attracted quite a following, including me!

One can achieve FIRE a plethora of ways—with frugality, geoarbitrage, saving 25x your annual expenses, real estate, side hustles, and so forth. Even so, a large number of Americans find FIRE unrealistic given the financial challenges of today's world. People think FIRE is just for DINKs (dual income, no kids) making six figures, living in extremely low cost-of-living areas, who can afford to save and scrimp and retire by 40. But I'm here to tell you, *anyone,* living *anywhere,* on almost *any* income can achieve FIRE. In *Passive Income, Aggressive Retirement,* I highlight one FIRE strategy in particular—it's the one that I argue is relevant and doable for *everyone.* It's the one that will restore your hope.

Henry David Thoreau once said, "The mass of men lead lives of quiet desperation."[1] I imagine he would be sorry to find that this quote still rings true, 173 years later. When I think about the general sentiment of today's generations, quiet desperation comes to mind.

We want to be financially independent and free to do what we want, but we see no way to make that happen. Instead (temporarily, we might tell ourselves), we've agreed to work long days for the next forty years of our lives only to *possibly* be able to retire. We've accepted limited vacation time and weekends that fly by in return for a much-needed paycheck. What choice do we have? We have student loans, seemingly never-ending bills due, kids to support, college funds to fill, and dogs to rush to the vet when they, once again, eat half a tennis ball.

Even retiring at age 65 seems unrealistic! A number has been circulating. That number is $2,000,000. That's how much money "the experts" say millennials will need to retire by age 65. Two million dollars. Like it's supposed to be easy or something. Sorry, but how many multi-millionaires do *you* know? This goal is not only highly unlikely but also unrealistic in this day and age, and I'll show you exactly why.

CNBC reports that 1 in 3 Americans have less than $5,000 saved for retirement.[2] They also report that baby boomers—you know, the ones who are literally about to retire?—have a median savings level of $24,280.[3]

Great. That cohort will last six whole months into their retirement before returning to work.

I'm not sure about you, but I don't feel optimistic about working in a cubicle, budgeting, and pinching pennies for 40 years in a sad attempt to save a couple mil.

News flash: traditional retirement is out. It's debunked. It's old news. (See Chapter 2 for details.)

So, what are we left with? It turns out that there's more than one way to FIRE.

My dear friend, allow me to introduce you to the revolutionary concept of **passive income**. Passive income is money that is earned with little to no work.

Sound impossible? Consider this: You put $10,000 in an online high-yield savings account that pays you 2% annual percentage yield (APY) per year. Over the year, you earn $200 in interest income. Did you have to do anything to earn that income? No! It's passive income.[4] AKA unearned income.

What if you had enough passive income to replace your earned income? Let's add three more zeros to the above example. If you put $10 million into that account, you'd make $200,000 per year in passive income. If you were collecting $200,000 per year in interest without lifting a finger, it would probably be safe to quit your day job.

Chances are, you don't have a cool $10 million sitting around, and neither did I. But there are hundreds of ways to make passive income, and many don't require any capital investment.

Who am I, and why am I qualified to reveal these secrets to you? My name is Rachel Richards. I'm 27 years old, retired, and living off $10,000+ per month in passive income. My husband, Andrew, and I now spend our time traveling the world, visiting friends and family, learning new skills, going on adventures, and doing whatever the hell we want.

When Andrew and I met, neither of us had any passive income, and we certainly weren't making enough to pursue FIRE otherwise. At that time, I was in a job for which I was overqualified and underpaid, working under a manager I despised—the dark days.

At age 24, I had several things going for me: I had no debt, something I am very proud of, as I worked my a$$ off in college selling knives (yeah,

Cutco)! Having majored in Financial Economics and worked as a financial advisor after college, I was frugal and savvy with my money. I was dating a like-minded man who also had no debt (Andrew used his military benefits to pay for tuition) and who was as open-minded and ambitious as I was. I also finally escaped that awful job and began a career at an amazing company on the greatest team ever, which made me feel pretty optimistic about climbing the corporate ladder.

My foray into passive income began with investing in real estate. From what I read and learned, owning property and collecting rent seemed like a fantastic way to build long-term wealth. My goal was to own a rental property, stat, and Andrew was on board.

At the time, I hadn't even put the concept of passive income together: real estate investing was just a thing I wanted to do, and little did I know I would soon discover FOUR other categories of passive income.

The next two years were a whirlwind. In 2017, Andrew and I bought our first duplex together; it cash-flowed $500 per month. We started a print-on-demand T-shirt business that generated passive royalties. I published my first book, *Money Honey: A Simple 7-Step Guide for Getting Your Financial $hit Together*, which also produced passive royalties. We bought several additional rental properties that year and the next, and by the end of 2018, we were over the $10,000 per month mark. These are just a couple examples of a plethora of passive income streams (which I will teach you about in this book), and we focused all of our efforts on growing them as much as possible. During those two years, we worked harder than we ever have in our lives.

I never dreamed of leaving my career until three things happened. First, Andrew and I started talking about moving out west, which was a problem because our jobs were in Louisville, KY. Second, we realized the importance of spending more time with the people we love, but we didn't have the flexibility to do so. And third, a dear manager asked me, "What do you actually want to do with your life?" I was stumped because I had no clear answer. This was a question I'd never considered. I'd always imagined I would climb the corporate ladder and become the CFO of a company someday.

But it occurred to me that because of my passive income streams, I had a choice. I had already more than replaced my full-time income. I didn't *have* to work anymore. I could follow my dreams of traveling the world, hiking ALL the things, writing, and using my unique financial skills and ideas to help others attain the same freedom we have. The ultimate decision to leave was nerve-racking, but I finally came to terms with what I wanted.

In 2019, a mere 2.5 years after our first duplex purchase, I handed in my notice and said, "Sayonara, baby" to my employer.

Andrew, whose passion truly is his career, has chosen to continue working remotely. His job is more fun for him these days since he works because he wants to, not because he has to.

Ever since I resigned from my career, I've been living in an alternate reality, a dream life. I am free to do whatever I want, whenever I want. I'm typing these words from the Rocky Mountains. Andrew is next to me, looking up real estate listings and listening to *Ready Player One* on Audible. We are munching on fresh apples and strawberries after our latest hike. We don't know what we'll do tonight, tomorrow, or five months from now because we have the freedom to make it up as we go. Money is never a worry. $10,000 per month in passive income alone is more than enough to cover our $7,000 per month in expenses; we live a flexible, enjoyable lifestyle and don't hold back. We are *free*. And words can't describe the liberation and joy we feel every day.

If we can go from $0 to $10,000 per month in passive income in under three years, so can you.

Even if you're not trying to retire early, maybe an extra $1,000, $2,000, or $5,000 per month *would* make a difference to you. Whether it pays your bills, is spent on hobbies or travel that you never thought you could afford, or is stashed away for a rainy day, you're inspired by the prospect of earning more each month. Passive income isn't all about quitting your job. The biggest benefits are:

Freedom.

Flexibility.

Financial independence.

I am positive that every single American adult has something to gain—not just financially, but emotionally and mentally—from supplemental, self-sustaining income.

Maybe you're a stay-at-home parent, and the idea of generating an income stream for your family excites you. Maybe you manage your money well but still have tens of thousands of student loan debt, and that extra income could help you accelerate your debt payoff. Maybe you are passionate about a career that pays poorly and need a way to supplement your income besides trading your time for money.

*I am positive that every single American adult has something to gain—not just financially, but emotionally and mentally—from supplemental, self-sustaining income.*

Regardless of your WHY, passive income could be your HOW.

If you regularly feel the Sunday Scaries or always dread getting up for work in the morning, this book is for you. This book is for the college student already dreading the 9-5 life that awaits them upon graduating; the couple who would rather spend their time doing what they want, instead of slaving away for their employers every day; and the frugal manager who has saved every penny for the last 15 years but still won't be able to retire for another 20 years.

If any of these scenarios resonate with you, then what awaits you in these pages will not only change your entire approach to life, but will also enable you to finally free yourself and start doing things for YOU and not for someone else. Once you take action with what you learn in this book, you will be on your way to financial independence.

In *Passive Income, Aggressive Retirement* (*PIAR*), I'll show you how we've all been tricked into thinking that working 40 hours per week for 40 years is natural and feasible. You will see how times have changed and that now, more than ever, young people are pushing back and demanding more out of life. You'll learn about the alternative, the solution, the way you can avoid being a cog in a corporation for the rest of your life.

Let me be clear: passive income isn't an easy way out. It's not a walk in the park; it takes sweat equity and sometimes money to create. If you think those two years were easy for me, well, SMH.[5] Nothing in life is easy, but if you had to choose between working your a$$ off for two years and retiring vs. trudging along for thirty years and retiring, which would you choose? If the latter sounds appealing, you should probably put this book down and go back to your cubicle. But if you are ready to do whatever it takes so that you can live out the rest of your life free from constraints, then keep reading. I'll give you the know-how; it's up to you to implement it. You *can* do this.

In *PIAR*, I have segmented passive income into five main categories, with many specific ideas within each category.

In Section One, you'll learn about how we have traditionally defined retirement and how times have changed. I'll introduce the beauty that is passive income: what it is and how it works. Next, we get into the five main categories of passive income and how to start building them:

Section Two: Royalty Income

Section Three: Portfolio Income

Section Four: Coin-Operated Machines

Section Five: Ads and E-Commerce

Section Six: Rental Income

And finally, in Section Seven, we wrap it all up by defining your goals, creating a strategy, and starting your passive income journey.

Join the thousands of people who have already found success with these strategies. All it takes is an eager beaver who is equal parts tenacious and creative.

Without further ado, let's do this.

# SECTION ONE:

# Introducing the Secret to Financial Independence

# CHAPTER 1

# *Times Are A-Changin'*

Ladles and Jellyspoons, the entire premise of this book is based on the idea that traditional retirement does not work anymore, so it is essential to understand what we mean when we say traditional retirement. How have we defined retirement over the last century? How has that looked? How have people achieved it?

Traditionally, people have subscribed to what I call the "Nest Egg Theory." A nest egg is a sum of money saved for the future. Fun fact: the term originates from the practice of putting a fake egg into a hen's nest to encourage her to lay.

The Nest Egg Theory formally goes like this: save a bajillion dollars by the time you retire and live off that for the rest of your life.

There is no doubt that the Nest Egg Theory has worked wonders in the past, and the purpose of this chapter is to show you why. Without this crucial piece of understanding, it would be easy to become frustrated with how dire retirement might seem in this day and age. And I don't want you turning bitter!

After you witness the evolution of what was once a fabulous retirement strategy, you will understand exactly why the concept of passive income is so brilliant and why it works so much better today.

## Did the Nest Egg Theory Ever Work?

Let's address the elephant in the room when it comes to the Nest Egg Theory. Why were we all led to believe that saving an enormous nest egg and retiring at age 65 would be a reasonable thing to do? Did this ever actually work?

The answer is that it worked splendidly... decades ago. The Nest Egg Theory was once easily attainable. Let's take a walk back in time and check out the year 1950. Since 1950, seven primary factors have drastically changed:

1) Household Expenses
2) Lifestyle Pressure
3) Life Expectancy
4) Social Security
5) Pensions
6) Cost of College
7) Hours Worked Per Week

I'll take you through these factors one at a time, showing you exactly how much the times have changed since 1950.

## Household Expenses

Americans have more housing today than ever before. The average single-family house in 1950 was 983 square feet.[6] Today, it's 2,641 square feet.[7]

Not only that, but the average family size in 1950 was 3.8 and the average family size in 2017 was 2.5.[8]

So, in 1950, each individual had 259 square feet to themselves, and today we each get 1,056 square feet. Holy moly! Why do we need all that space? (There's so much room for activities!)

Because houses are getting bigger, we are spending a lot more money on housing today than we did decades ago. The same trend applies to cars and technology. A family in 1950 might get by on one car that was shared by all; a family today normally has one car per adult. Also, technological needs are pretty much mandatory these days. Every household needs at least one computer, and all working-aged people need a cell phone.

One of the most significant contributions to money troubles for families these days is the cost of childcare. Finding data about the cost of childcare in the 1950s is difficult because most moms in a two-parent household stayed home with kids. In 1956, 16% of women with children under 6 worked outside the home.[9] In more recent years, labor force participation among moms with preschool-aged children stands at 64%.[10] Also, getting your baby into a decent daycare often requires getting on the waiting list while you're trying to conceive! When childcare costs are through the roof, moms can't win: they must either work to afford it, leave the workforce to avoid the expense, or juggle it all.

A higher quality of life is what we strive for with each new generation, but with that can come higher costs, which can mean a lesser ability to save money for retirement.

## Lifestyle Pressure

These days, kids, teens, and adults are inundated with online pictures portraying a perfect lifestyle. Advertisements show models driving Ferraris and living in high-rises in New York City. Heck, I regularly see online acquaintances driving fancy sports cars and living in crazy-nice places.

Keeping up with the Joneses used to mean being jealous of your neighbor who just bought a Porsche and wanting to do the same. It was geographically limited to who was literally within eyesight of you. Social media has changed the world. It can make us feel like we deserve certain things in life just because we see thousands of other people having them. Back in 1950, when the Internet didn't exist, this type of lifestyle pressure didn't exist—at least, not to the extent it does today.

Everything centers around beauty. Our kitchens can no longer be just functional; they must be tastefully designed and decorated. Laundry isn't tucked away in unfinished basements or garages anymore; our matching washing machines and dryers are now presented in our flawlessly organized mudroom. Ugliness is not to be tolerated! I know people who are even embarrassed by their home because it's not "beautiful" enough. Everything must be #Instagrammable.

Psychologically, it's more difficult than ever before to refrain from spending our money when all it takes to justify our next purchase is the thought, "If my high school friend Samantha, who surely doesn't make as much as I do, can afford it, then I can too."

## Life Expectancy

Someone of retirement age in 1950 was expected to live to age 79.[11] Someone of retirement age today is expected to live to age 83.[12] That means today's retirees need to fund an additional four years of retirement!

Not only are we living longer, but we are also retiring earlier. In 1940 the average retirement age was 70, and in 2000 it was 62.[13]

So, what does all this mean? Our retirement length has increased dramatically. Male workers in 1950 had an average retirement length of eight years, as compared to *19 years* today! Bottom line: we need WAY more money than ever before to retire.

## Social Security

Luckily (or unluckily) for you, when I was in college, I wrote my senior thesis on Social Security, so forgive me if I get a bit zealous here. In the United States, Social Security is a program that provides government benefits to retired, unemployed, or disabled people. If you're a fellow millennial or Gen Zer, chances are you've heard rumors about Social Security not even being around by the time we retire. This begs the question: what on earth happened?

A brief history lesson: Our good ole President Franklin D. Roosevelt (FDR) signed the Social Security Act of 1935. The need for government benefits was largely due to the Great Depression, and the aid was vital for many families. Problem: the government didn't have a way to fund this new program. It would take an enormous amount of money to begin giving cash to every retired and disabled person in the States. The government's solution was to set up a system in which the younger generations fund the older generations' retirement benefits. FDR implemented the Social

Security tax on currently *working* Americans. That tax revenue was then used to pay for the currently *retired* Americans.[14]

So that 6.2% Social Security tax that gets withdrawn from each paycheck? That's not set aside somewhere for YOU; it's used right now to pay for currently retired Americans.[15]

This setup was an ingenious idea. The working Americans in the first several decades of Social Security vastly outnumbered retired Americans. For each retired person collecting Social Security, there were multiple working people paying into Social Security. In 1940, the year the first benefits were paid out, there were 159.4 workers per covered beneficiary.[16] Setting up the tax this way meant that there would be more than enough money for retired Americans.

...Until things changed.

The baby boomer generation, i.e., the people who were born roughly between the years of 1946 to 1964, quickly became the largest generation in America at that time. This was fantastic. When they reached working age and began contributing to Social Security, the trust fund ballooned!

What the government failed to account for was that the baby boomer population would eventually retire. And that when they inevitably began to retire, the impact would be devastating because there would be fewer working Americans per retired American. In 2013, there were only 2.8 workers per covered beneficiary.[16]

The decline in the number of children per family is another alarming trend when it comes to Social Security. Fewer babies being born today means the size of that workforce will be smaller. A smaller workforce has a harder time supporting the larger retired population.

The changes in demographics began to put an enormous financial strain on the program. Suddenly, there were so many retired people receiving benefits that the fund's surplus was shrinking day by day.

Sure, the govt has slightly pushed back the retirement date, increased the tax, and lowered benefits over time—but not quickly or drastically enough.

The Trustees recently published a "message to the public," summarizing the 2019 annual reports. "Over the program's 84-year history, it has collected roughly $21.9 trillion and paid out $19.0 trillion, leaving asset reserves of $2.9 trillion at the end of 2018 in its two trust funds."

Cause for celebration? Not quite. They go on to say that the trust funds will be fully depleted in 2035. Additionally, Social Security's total cost is projected to exceed its total income (including interest) in 2020 for the first time since 1982.[17] Peachy.

What was once an admirable, rock-solid social insurance program is now a hot mess. The size of aging generations is putting an enormous strain on the program, and the funds are being rapidly depleted. Not only is the baby boomer generation (inadvertently) causing pressure, but so is their increased life expectancy and earlier retirement age.

> " *admirable, rock-solid social insurance program* "

All this boils down to the fact that millennials today are paying for the retirement of their boomer parents via Social Security taxes. But when millennials want to retire? As it stands, they're SOL.[18] It could be wise to prepare for the worst-case scenario and not count on reaping *any* Social Security benefits at all when you retire if you're currently under 40 years of age.

## Pensions

Pensions are quickly becoming a thing of the past. A pension is a type of defined-benefit plan offered by employers or the government. It works like this: in exchange for a long and loyal tenure at a company, that company pays you a monthly sum of money from the time you retire until the time you die. And that's on top of any Social Security benefits for which you qualify. Nifty!

For the reasons listed in the Social Security section above, pensions are going extinct, and the ones that still exist today often aren't even that great. Pensions became too costly for employers to maintain, so decades ago, Corporate America began lobbying Congress to offer a new type of retirement benefit. That's where 401(K)s came into place, and 401(K)s have quickly taken over as the most commonly-used employer-sponsored plan.

The difference with a 401(K) is that the employee is responsible for contributing to it. Many employees don't have the self-discipline or ability to take advantage of that fully. 401(K)s place the burden of retirement on the employee instead of the employer.

Gone are the days of defined-benefit plans and the safety net of a pension.

## Cost of College

Raise your hand if you can relate to the following meme:

*Thank you, student loans, for getting me through college.*

*I don't think I can ever repay you.*

One of the most widely reported trends from 1950 until today is the rising cost of college.

A 2018 Forbes article stated, "The cost of a college education is skyrocketing. It's no surprise that student loans now make up the largest chunk of U.S. non-housing debt. Yes, more than both credit cards or auto loans."[19]

A little comparison, if you will. In the 1988-1989 academic year, the tuition and fees of a public four-year college cost $3,360 (in 2018 dollars). That's a total of about $13,000 over four years. In the 2018-2019 academic year, those same four years cost over $40,000![20] That's more than TRIPLE the price in only thirty years. And you don't even want to *know* the numbers for private colleges.

My dad, a good ole Kentucky boy, worked in a tobacco warehouse each summer and tutored during the school years to pay for his private college, which cost him about $3,200 per year at the time. Doable, right? Many boomers like him remember working their way through college with ease and graduating with little to no debt.

Here's what Papa Richards has to say: "The job I landed upon graduation paid $14,500, which was more than I paid for all four years of college. Those ratios are vastly different today. How many new graduates can find a job today with starting pay that is more than their total cost of college? The ROI is different."

Oh, by the way, I went to the same college my dad attended. 35 years later, it cost me about $42,000 per year. My degree cost over $150,000 more than his did. Love that for me.

Graduating without debt is virtually impossible now. Current students can't just get a summer job and expect to earn enough to pay for tuition. Don't get me wrong; some students find a way, and that's highly impressive. But for the vast majority of us, graduating without debt isn't realistic unless someone is helping foot the bill or they've racked up some serious scholarship money.

With the cost so exorbitantly high, and everyone and their neighbor attending undergrad, a college degree is less advantageous these days.

When you think about the financial impact of graduating with debt, we are actually *negating our goal* of creating income streams. Debt generates *negative cash flow each month*. Once those student loan payments kick in, they're already a drain on income that could last for several decades. For the purpose of this book, we're trying to *create* $700 a month in passive income, not *pay* a $700 monthly debt payment.

## Hours Worked Per Week

Back in the 1800s, the vast majority of the workforce was in factories, where ten- and eleven-hour workdays, seven days per week, were the norm. Luckily, one special dude changed all that during the Roaring Twenties: Henry Ford. Ford is widely credited for introducing the 40-hour workweek in 1926. He believed that too many hours adversely affected employees' productivity.[21] The 40-hour workweek was a huge win for employees, and other companies were pressured to follow suit.

But if there's one thing that hasn't changed at all since 1950, it's the 40-hour workweek. In fact, a 2014 Gallup poll showed that the average hours worked per week was more like 47; essentially six days instead of five.[22]

When I asked my friends what they thought of the 40-hour week, one said, "I would LOVE a 40-hour workweek! I often work 50-60 hours per week." Case in point.

Is it time to question our society's devotion to the 40-hour week? "After all, the standard American workweek, which traces its roots to the industrial age, may be ill-suited for a knowledge-based economy," states Theresa Agovino, an NYC-based business writer.[23] Our country is a lot different now than it was a century ago when the concept was first widely implemented.

I sought feedback from my network regarding the 40-hour workweek. Here's what they had to say:

"I'd rather be evaluated by outcome." -Amy

"It's an outdated notion. In my previous job, I'd get all my work accomplished in about the equivalent of 30 hours, and I'd honestly spend 10 hours doing absolutely worthless stuff." -Tina

"I'd totally love a three-day weekend... Give me Friday or Monday off, and I would be a happy camper." -Katelyn

"I truly think it depends on what your line of work is." -Ingrid

"I HATE it... it makes me feel so trapped and unproductive. Hold me accountable in different ways, but don't force me to sit in an office for 40 hours a week." -Tori

"I think it should be more output-based. Some people work faster than others. If I finish two hours early and have nothing left for the day, why can't I go home and relax?" -Chelsea

"I definitely think [the 40-hour week] is an outdated concept that was developed back when work was consistent every day and more hours put in meant that more work was done (think of farming, assembly lines, production for retail, etc.)" -Elisabeth

"The 40-hour workweek is so irrelevant. Who cares how many hours you work as long as you accomplish what you need to, preferably exceeding expectations?" -Carrie

My own experience is in line with this feedback. At more than one job, I often went through weeks of busyness and chaos, followed by weeks of calm and boredom. I was frustrated when one manager told me that it didn't look good if I left work at 4:45 pm every day, despite coming in at 7:30 am and not taking lunch. That manager emphasized that I should be trying to create proper *perceptions*. That feedback in itself was proof that my supervisors valued hours put in *over* output. In their eyes, longer hours worked equated to a better employee.

Suffice to say, the vast majority of people I know are less-than-pleased with this work arrangement. Unfortunately, there's a lingering perception that anything less than 40 hours is lazy and inadequate.

A 2018 Deloitte survey reported that flexibility is key to millennial and Gen Z loyalty. "Those who are less than satisfied with their pay and work flexibility are increasingly attracted to the gig economy."[24]

Workers are asking for change, but companies aren't responding. "At this point, if you get all your work done in 30 hours, all that is going to happen is that someone is going to give you more work to do," says Claire Bissot, managing director at CBIZ HR Services.[23]

Millennials became the largest generation in the labor force in 2016. They, along with Gen Z, are demanding change. The 40-hour workweek feels more oppressive than ever before.

## Conclusion

I've given you seven of the most significant factors that have changed over time, but there are certainly more. The point is that our economic landscape has changed, and none of the changes are making this whole retirement thing easier.

A young couple in the 1950s had a lot going for them. They probably owned a 1,000 square foot house and shared one car. Yes, there was some Keeping-Up-With-The-Joneses pressure, but they weren't constantly inundated with social media pictures of strangers' gorgeous kitchens and luxurious vacations. The husband worked full-time while the wife stayed home to raise the kids, and they expected to retire at age 66. Not only did they never need student loans, but they expected their children to be able to pay for their education on their own as well. The husband and wife would be able to count on Social Security to supplement the husband's pension during retirement. Plus, they had their nest egg of money they'd been saving their whole lives for an extra cushion.

Compare this to a similar family now. A young couple owns a 2,000 square foot house and two cars. They both work full-time and will be paying off their student loans for years to come. Their only other debt is their mortgage, but they're still not sure how they will afford to send their kids to college. They don't have nearly enough savings to last them through a 30-year retirement, they are reluctant to count on Social Security benefits, and their employers don't offer a pension. They feel that they have done all the right things and are still falling short.

Admittedly, these scenarios are fictional and aren't 100% representative of every couple or family. There are so many more factors, so I know this is a simplistic view of things, but it should still give you a sense of how much has changed between then and now. Retiring used to be relatively straightforward.

But hello?! What worked in 1950 does not work today! At some point along the line, we failed to account for all these changing trends. What are we left with?

We are left with a totally outdated retirement philosophy. What once was realistic does not work anymore, and doing the same things we did decades ago will only set us up for failure.

> *What was once realistic does not work anymore, and doing the same things we did decades ago will only*
> **"**

But, do changing times completely void the Nest Egg theory? Maybe it can still work for most of us, right?

No way, José. In the next chapter, we'll zero in on the Nest Egg theory itself so you can see precisely how risky and difficult it can be. Once we've myth-busted the Nest Egg theory, we'll finally make way for the means to financial independence, via passive income.

CHAPTER 2

# Nest Egg Theory, Debunked

**R**etirement definitions:

"Withdrawal from one's position or occupation or from active working life." –Merriam-Webster

"The action or fact of leaving one's job and ceasing to work." –Dictionary.com

"The period of life when one chooses to permanently leave the workforce behind." –Investopedia

The definitions above are pretty consistent, but what do you think it means to be retired? How would you define it? Does it have to do with freedom or financial independence? Is it simply the act of quitting your job and never working again? Can you "retire" and still work?

I asked my friend how she would define retirement, and she said, "Not having to work at all anymore." What does her definition imply?

Traditionally, you work because you need money. You wouldn't survive without your paycheck, at least not for long. So, if retirement means not having to work at all anymore, then the definition implies financial independence.

Retirement = freedom.

Retirement = choice.

Retirement = financial independence.

*of retirement implies financial*

If you're financially independent, you can do whatever the hell you want! Maybe you want to keep working—great! The point is that you'll now work because you want to, not because you have to. You're not working for the money anymore. To be clear, in this book, "early retirement" and "financial independence" are interchangeable. They mean the same thing.

## Two Million Dollars

The definition of retirement is one thing, the "how" is another. And for the last century, we have all subscribed to the Nest Egg theory: save an enormous amount of money to live off of when you retire. How much money would say, a millennial need for such a scenario?

Doing a quick Google search shows that the oft-cited retirement nest egg millennials must attain is, oh, just $2 mil.

For instance, in 2016, Robert Powell of USA Today stated that older millennials would need $1.8 million, and younger millennials would need upwards of $2.5 million to retire comfortably.[25] In early 2019, Farm Bureau Financial Services wrote that while baby boomers needed $1.3 million to retire, millennials will need $1.8 million.[26] The reason for the higher amount? Lower Social Security benefits, paired with inflation. Other experts, such as John Rampton from Entrepreneur.com, cite figures as high as $7 million.[27] For the purposes of this book, I'll go somewhere on the modest side and say the average amount a millennial will need for retirement at age 65 is $2 million.

In reality, how often are people successful at saving that amount?

Baby boomers might not need $2 million, but they certainly need more than what they actually have saved. A 2016 study showed that the mean retirement account savings of people in the 56-61 age bracket was only $163,577.[28] A 2015 study found that fifty-something workers have a total household savings of $117,000 and most plan to work past age 65 or not retire at all.[29] In fact, according to the Government Accountability Office (GAO), around 29% of households age 55 and older have neither retirement savings nor a pension.[30]

Say what? Is there something wrong here, or have millennials been bamboozled into thinking that saving $2,000,000 is doable? Especially when baby boomers don't even have a tenth of that saved! The stats paint a shocking reality; very few people will manage to hit that number.

What would it take to save two million dollars? Starting at age 25, you'd need to save about $621 per month for forty years, assuming 8% annually compounded interest. I don't know about you, but most millennials I know straight up can't afford that... Not on a $40,000 salary with $400 student loan payments, at least. Saving $2 mil is not easy, and it's not something you take for granted. Unfortunately, most of us will never get there.

I'm not sure why this retirement method is fed to us by the media, by our parents and teachers and friends, and even by financial gurus such as Suze Orman and Dave Ramsey. Don't get me wrong; I'm an enormous Dave Ramsey fan. I just find it ironic that these gurus teach other people how to get rich by saying things like "pay off debt" and "save 15% of your income" when the gurus themselves got rich by selling products and being business owners.

Maybe you're feeling optimistic, though. Maybe you don't have student loan debt, credit card debt, or a car payment. That was my situation when I graduated from college, so I know it's possible, and a few of you are out there. I can already see the cogs turning in your head, calculating how you can achieve this $2 million goal.

## Limits to Saving More Money
You'll have to save a lotta money. Hint: there are precisely two ways to do so.

1) Decrease your expenses

2) Increase your income

We tend to instinctively focus on cutting expenses when we want to save more money rather than increasing income.

The problem with focusing only on expenses is twofold:

1) It's limited. You can only cut your costs so much. Generally, things like mortgage payments and utility bills are non-negotiable (although it doesn't hurt to try! Let me know how it goes.)

2) It's unsustainable. Can you say, "Goodbye, quality of life?" Never going out for drinks, never buying a new shirt, never traveling. "That's appealing!" said no one ever. When you budget so strictly, the budget won't last. It's frustrating to permanently lower your quality of life by cutting out things you enjoy. I'm not saying you shouldn't monitor your expenses; if you've read my book *Money Honey*, you'll know how important it is to get your spending under control.

We are all familiar with the common financial advice:

Friend: *"I can't get my spending under control."*

You: *"Track your spending so you can see what you are spending too much on. Then create a budget and stick to it!"*

Friend: *"What should I invest in?"*

You: *"A mix of stocks and bonds. But not just one stock, make sure to pick lots of different ones or a mutual or index fund so that you are diversified."*

Yes: the basics of money management are important. I teach these things in *Money Honey*, and I stand by them to this day. These skills are vital for managing your money well on a day-to-day basis. But ain't nobody ever gonna save $2,000,000 by cutting back on their daily Starbucks and investing their money in mutual funds. It's going to take a lot more than that.

## You Can't Control the Stock Market

The stock market makes no promises that even if you managed to save that $621 per month for 40 years, you'd get an 8% return. You can't control the stock market. It goes up on its own, it goes down on its own, and you cannot predict what it will do, ever. And if your timing is less than ideal, and you're a 62-year-old that's too heavily invested when the next recession hits... there goes your nest egg. Tragically, that was the fate for many Americans who were about to retire in 2008 and 2009. It will take them years, even decades, to make up their loss.

How would you feel if that were you? You did everything right: you paid off your debt, you were frugal, you said "no" time and time again to travel plans or dinners out, you scrimped and saved, and here you finally are, ready to retire with your $2 million, only to lose half of it. If you are nearing retirement age and strongly invested in the stock market during a recession period, you are $hit outta luck. Retirement plans = cancelled. Indefinitely.

The stock market isn't the only thing that could cause you to lose your fortune. Anything unexpected or out of your control could wipe away your savings. I'm talking divorce, a long-term disability, a lawsuit, or medical problems. Enter any one of those four, and you can kiss your nest egg goodbye.

In short, even if you do all the right things, your life savings aren't guaranteed.

## Escaping the Rat Race

In my early twenties, I set up a plan to save $2,000,000 by age sixty or so. But after a while, I began to think through all the potential risks outlined above. I also took a good, hard look at the forty years ahead of me. And I realized I wanted out.

I'm not the only one who has felt less-than-turned-on by the idea of working my whole life for a retirement that could be swept away at any moment. I asked for some feedback online regarding what it means, emotionally, to be retired. Here are a few of the responses I received:

"When you can afford to stop doing the job you do to afford to live." – Kelly

"Having enough saved to be 9-5 free." –Beth

"The time in life where you're living and no longer surviving." –Holli

"Sweet, sweet freedom." –Kasey

"Something that doesn't come soon enough." -Elizabeth

These responses all have one thing in common: an implied feeling of being trapped and not truly enjoying life.

Think about it: most of us are working a full-time job in exchange for a salary. We signed our lives away *to make someone else's dreams come true*. The CEO and shareholders are getting fat and happy, and what are we getting for all our efforts? We are likely working 40-but-really-almost-50-hour weeks. We work five days so that we can enjoy two weekend days. What is the ROI on that? You put in five, and you get out two... it's not looking good, buddy. How much vacation do you get? Two weeks, three weeks if you have a generous employer? When you negotiated your job offer, you signed a dotted line saying you'd trade 49 weeks of your life so that you could enjoy three weeks off. Per year. And you were most likely happy about it.

Are you scratching your head?

Would you ever give someone $49 and accept $3 in return? No. So why are you treating your time that way? That's your *life* you are trading. Why do we think it's acceptable to work our whole life and only get to play when we're 65? Just because everyone else is doing it? Just because "that's how it is"?

I don't think so.

## Gloom & Doom

If you're still not convinced, don't worry, I'll keep going. Let's discuss death for a second.

You are not even guaranteed to live until age 65.

Yes, you are likely to live to age 65. We live in a first-world country, we have some of the world's best doctors and hospitals, and chances are, you're not an adrenaline junkie or the guy from "Free Solo." But—and this is an enormous but—there are no guarantees in life. Not even life itself. Rather than embark down the clichéd "life is short" narrative, I want to ask you something. Is it worth the risk? Is it worth slaving away your whole life and putting off your freedom when there's a chance you might not ever even get to enjoy that freedom?

If you do reach retirement age, there's no promise that you will be in good health. Strokes, heart attacks, and cancer become more common as you age. No matter how healthy you are, you can't always control your health.

At this moment, you are the youngest (and therefore, likely the most physically fit) you will ever be. Don't you want to do things like play with your kids with unlimited energy and run a marathon in your twenties and thirties and forties? Personally, I can't see myself ⟨ ⟩ camp at the ripe old age of 70... I probably wouldn't even want to. It doesn't make sense to wait until you're in your sixties to go on adventures and to do things that require you to be at your physical best.

*guarantees in life.*

*Not even life itself.*

Listen, ladies and gents, this plan is enormously flawed. Let's re-cap the problems of the Nest Egg Theory:

1) Saving $2,000,000 is hard; you can only cut your expenses so much

2) You can't control the stock market

3) You could experience a divorce, death, long-term disability, lawsuit, or medical emergency

4) Working for 40 years is not appealing

5) You could die and not ever reach retirement

6) You could become ill and not able to fully enjoy retirement

Yikes. This strategy has way too many ifs, ands, and buts for you to actually feel secure. I mean, *everything* would have to go right for it to work out.

So please, can we finally lay this theory to rest? It's not a good plan. We've been brainwashed into thinking that not only is saving for retirement possible, but "*it's easy! Just save 15% of each paycheck.*" No, no, NO.

Allow reality to seep into your bones and urge you into action. You must change your perspective on this. Let me guide you into the light!

## Younger Generations are Waking Up

Either you were already thinking this before you bought this book or you agree with it now, but younger generations are finally beginning to realize that retiring ain't so easy. Not only that, but they don't want to devote their entire lives to an unfulfilling career in a lame attempt to save up $2,000,000.

This realization has resulted in three distinct responses:

1) The "This is my reality" or "I'm okay with settling" response. Essentially, young people have numbingly accepted the Nest Egg theory and the dire outlook of their next forty years as reality. There's no way around it, so might as well trudge along and go through the motions. These people might even have some hope that they can live frugally enough to make it to retirement. They might even follow and implement some of the recent movements focused on frugality: Mustachianism, Minimalism, and the Tiny House movement. Maybe buying into these concepts and living frugally enough will be sufficient, maybe it won't. Either way, this cohort has settled for what they view as their only way forward.

2) The "Why bother?" response. These people see the dire circumstances for exactly what they are, and they feel hopeless. They don't see the point of even trying to scrape enough savings together while working a meaningless 9-5 job, so in a desperate attempt to glean some pleasure from life, they've given up trying to be frugal at all. This attitude leads to complete financial irresponsibility and possibly even a sense of entitlement, or just bitterness at the world and the way things are. They think, "Might as well live big and spend my money now since I'll be screwed no matter what I do."

3) The "F that" response. These are the people that have looked for an alternative option. They refuse to accept this reality and are determined to find a better way. They are pursuing FIRE on their terms. Surely there is some 3rd solution, some unthought-of option that has not yet been explored? They think, "I'm going to find a better way to do this," and are determined to succeed.

I first identified with Response #1. But while I've always attempted to live frugally and be responsible with my money, the idea of downsizing my life drastically enough to pursue FIRE was a bit of a turn off to me. Besides, when I graduated from college, I was making $36,000. I was saving 50% of my income, an impressive feat. But even saving $18,000 per year would not guarantee traditional retirement, let alone early retirement! Are you kidding me?

Some of the methods to FIRE work great for those with high incomes, no kids, and who don't mind living a life of extreme frugality. They can save aggressively for five to ten years and retire in their thirties or forties. But let's face it: that level of savings is just not a practical or realistic path for most people. What about the single parent raising two kids on $50,000 per year? How much could that person save, *really?* Plus, is it worth giving up your quality of life that much when you're young? I'm not convinced.

Now, I'm in full-on Response #3. I have found the better way to financial independence, have proven it to work, and am making it my mission to educate others about it as well. Life doesn't have to be this way. We can choose the alternative, the 3rd solution.

At this point, you understand the lay of the land: how times have changed, why the Nest Egg Theory is the standard route to retirement, and why saving a $2 million nest egg is unrealistic. You've probably identified with some of the common reactions to this knowledge. The next step to pursuing the alternative solution is to understand our most valuable resource so that you can see why passive income is so brilliant.

# CHAPTER 3

# Your #1 Most Valuable Resource

Traditionally, we trade our time for money. We can't make money without putting in our time.

What happens when we make our income independent of our time? This chapter will explain the thought process that finally gets us to the passive income concept. We'll discuss two resources—time and money—and which one is more valuable. Then, we'll look at how being frugal and outsourcing work can help us prioritize our resources. Finally, we'll tie all these concepts together and relate them to passive income. You will see exactly why passive income is so powerful and how it frees up our most valuable resource.

Time or money: what is your most valuable resource?

If you could have more money or more time, which would you choose? Close this book (no looking ahead!) and take a few moments to finalize your answer in your mind.

For a research project, professors from the University of California posed this question to over 4,000 Americans and found that most people valued money over time.[31] But they also found that the people who chose *time* were "on average statistically happier and more satisfied with life than the people who chose money," even when all other variables were held constant.[32]

I was curious about what my own network would say, so I conducted an informal (read: Facebook) poll in a group of mostly young professional women. I asked them: "Time or money: Which is your most valuable resource, and why?" 90.2% said time, and 9.8% said money.

Not everyone has the choice of time vs. money in the first place. Systemic poverty forces many people to spend as many hours as possible taking extra shifts and doing everything in their power to make money just so they can survive. Actually, it doesn't even take poverty to be this way; it's impacting the middle class too. Not spending that extra time working could potentially mean that their bills don't get paid.

One of my poll responders, Gillian, made this important distinction: "There is a happy medium. Once you hit a wage that can support you and your [...]e." Another responder, Samantha, who [...]utlined how she was struggling to make [...]nds meet, said: "I choose money. It's so [p]recious to me right now that I can't not [c]hoose it, though I wish to God it weren't."

Some people do have a choice [b]etween more time or more money. And [e]ven more people may not think they have [th]e choice, but really, it's a matter of will. [M]ost of us who feel like we don't have [e]nough time (this is me, every day) or [m]oney, simply need to manage our time and [...] [o]tion of sacrificing something to free up time or money. We must recognize that yes, it is a sacrifice, but we can make it happen if we are determined enough.

> **"** *Everyone's time comes at a price, and every precious minute we spend is a minute we will NEVER get back.* **"**

Guys and gals, your most valuable resource is your time.

You can always make more money, but you can't make more time. We were all born on this planet with a single finite resource: time. We all have an end date. None of us can stop the clock from ticking. Everyone's time comes at a price, and every precious minute we spend is a minute we will NEVER get back.

The same cannot be said for money. There are always opportunities to make more money. Every dollar you spend IS replaceable, and you *can* get that dollar back.

If you have enough time, you can make more money. But no matter how much money you have, you can't make more time.

Time is the great equalizer. Warren Buffett does not have more time than you or me. In terms of time—in terms of *life*—we are all equal.

The idea that time is your most valuable resource is an important concept, and I challenge you to remind yourself of that every day. If you understand that, then you'll get why passive income is so brilliant.

## Frugality

When you think of people who live in extreme frugality, you might think of the Tiny House movement and Minimalism. Both are examples of consumers living frugally to become financially independent.

Being frugal means that you are economical in your consumption of *resources*. Notice I said resources, not money. We should not only focus on being frugal with our money, but also on being frugal with our time.

And if we've established that time is more valuable than money, then why aren't we acting in accordance with our values? Frugality is good, but not when we're trading time for money. So, how come I know so many people who will drive twenty minutes out of their way to get gas that's $0.10 cheaper per gallon? Why do people spend thirty minutes looking for coupons that will save them $1.50 at the store?

In making these choices, you are always *spending* something. You're either spending time or money.

Now I'm not saying, "Don't buy cheaper gas or use coupons." I'm just saying to not engage in activities that are not *worth* your time.

What is your time worth? Are you making $10 per hour? $20, $30, $70 per hour? Let's calculate how much your time is worth. We need to look at your total income from all sources and your total time spent on making that income to find your real hourly wage.

First, calculate your total time investment per week. Ensure that you account for all hours worked. Include time spent at your full-time job, side hustles, part-time gigs, and so forth. Add up the total time you spend working and making money each week. Write that down.

Next, tally up your total weekly income. Include income from all of your jobs and side hustles. Write that down.

Divide your total income by your total time spent to arrive at a per hour figure. This figure represents how much your time is worth.

I know people whose time is worth $30 per hour but will waste an hour driving to three different grocery stores to find the best prices in order to save ten bucks. But that doesn't make sense! If your time is worth $30 per hour, you wouldn't agree to spend an hour of your time to save $10. Yet people do it all the time. Even those who emphatically believe that their time is worth more than their money live in contradiction to their values with the choices they make. It may not even be a conscious choice; I *still* catch myself doing this. It's a lot easier said than done.

Whether they are aware of it or not, people often make these types of choices because they haven't calculated what their time is worth. To help decide between saving money or saving time, we all need to speak the same "currency." By evaluating both options in terms of dollars, the outcome becomes obvious.

Let's say you are working on your wedding invitations. You have all the products, and now you need to stuff the envelopes, write the addresses in neat handwriting, place stamps, and put them in the mail. You estimate that this will take you four hours. Alternatively, your niece has offered to do this for you for fifty bucks. What should you do?

First, calculate how much your time is worth. Let's say you make $700 per week at your full-time job, working 40 hours, and another $100 per week from your dog-walking gig, which takes you roughly three hours. In total, you make $800 per week for 43 hours of time. That's about $18.60 per hour.

Second, calculate the total cost of your time if you were to complete the project. If the project will take you four hours, it will "cost" you 4 x $18.60 = $74.40.

Finally, go with the cheaper option. You can either spend $74.40 of your own time or pay your niece $50. It will "cost you" less to hire your niece.

Now, in no world does it makes sense to outsource every task in your life so that you can sit your butt on the couch and stare at the wall instead. If you do that, your wallet will be hurting. You're not "saving" money in the example above if you take that four hours and watch Netflix. You must think in terms of *opportunity cost*. If you have extra time and no extra money, maybe DIYing the invites *is* the most efficient use of resources. The point is to make an educated decision with the way you are spending your time and money. Being informed is cool, y'all.

If saving time is important to you, then next time you have trouble with the time vs. money tradeoff, you can use this method to help you decide.

Not only have we argued that our time is more valuable than our money, but we now have a surefire method to ensure we are living by that value.

## Outsourcing

The wedding invitation scenario above is an example of outsourcing. Back in 2017, when Andrew and I were busting our butts working seventy hours per week, I was desperate to free up more time. I finally had an epiphany: outsource as many tasks as possible.

First thought: *We could hire cleaners and landscapers!*

Second thought: *Ew, Rachel! I'm supposed to be responsible with my money. Aren't those things a luxury? Why would I pay someone my hard-earned money when I could do it myself?*

Third thought: *Oh, wait. For $65 per week, someone could clean the whole house, saving me four hours on the weekend. Four hours of my time is worth over $200! This idea is a no-brainer... why didn't I do this before?*

We tried to outsource everything. The question we continued to ask ourselves was: "How else can we trade *money* for *time*?"

But it wasn't enough. We wanted the best of both worlds. We wanted more money, *and* we wanted more time.

## Passive Income is the Answer

This chapter started with the question, "Time or Money: Which is your most valuable resource?" But what if you didn't have to pick between the two at all? What if you could have more of both?

You'd have to find a way to make a self-sustaining income stream. Doing so would mean you could make money without working. You would be free to spend your time however you see fit. No longer trading your time for money has two benefits: A) you don't have to spend forty to fifty hours per week working, and B) you don't have to be physically present at an office or cubicle. You'd get to enjoy both freedom of time and freedom of location.

*cuts the link between time and money*

And that, friends, is the premise of passive income, or income that is maintained with little to no work. Passive income is the key to being free: Freeing up our time, freeing up the location we must be in, freeing up our lives from being financially dependent on our employer.

Passive income cuts the link between time and money.

If your passive income exceeds your expenses, you are retired. #MicDrop.

## Daydreaming of Retirement

Allow yourself to fantasize for a bit. Retirement, while having a literal definition, must have a deeper meaning to you. Yeah, okay, you won't have to work long, tiring weeks anymore. But what will you do? Have you ever thought about it? Going from workaholic to 16 hours of free time per day is quite a drastic change. Some retirees end up not liking it at all. They're bored, or they feel that their lives don't have a purpose anymore, or they feel like they're not adding value to the world. No one wants to retire just to sit around in their PJs, twiddling their thumbs all day. (I mean, I'll admit, that might be nice for a solid two weeks. Total sloth-like existence. Sign me up!)

You'll need to fill your time somehow. Thinking through this *now* will not only create more passion and determination to get to that point; it will eliminate any fear you might have of getting to that point. Having a plan is crucial.

Ideally, you'll fill your time doing something fulfilling to you. Fulfillment means different things to different people, so there's no right or wrong answer. You might already know what fulfills you. For me, it's educating people on money management and passive income. It's writing. It's building businesses. It's traveling. Other people might find fulfillment in raising kids, volunteering, coaching, or even a specific cause: spreading the word on climate change, educating people on the addictive effects of iPhone use among children, or banning plastic straws. Your imagination is the limit.

If you have no idea what fulfills you, consider the following questions:

If money didn't exist, how would you spend your time?

What would you do if you only had one year left to live?

If you won $20 million in the lottery, what would you do at first, and what would you do later?

# CHAPTER 4

# *Passive Income: Such Beauty, Such Grace*

First, my dear students, a vocabulary lesson. For the purposes of this book, I categorize everything into two types of income: active or passive. But keep in mind that the Internal Revenue Service (IRS) identifies a variety of income types, each with its own tax treatment. Please don't use my below definitions for your tax return.

Active Income: First, you have earned or active income, which you earn by working—by trading time for dollars (yuck). Active income is the only or primary source of income for most Americans. We provide our labor and services in exchange for dolla dolla bills y'all. You can be an independent contractor or an employee to earn an active income.

Active income is taxed at the highest rate, with a 2019 marginal tax rate of a whopping 37%. That means that at a certain point, for every $100 you make, the government takes $37 and leaves you with $63. But that's not all;

active income is also subjected to other taxes such as Social Security and Medicare.

Passive Income: On the other hand, the IRS considers passive income to include rental income plus any business activities in which the earner does not materially participate. My translation: passive income is income earned with little to no work. Passive income is the least taxed type of income.

Also, in *Passive Income, Aggressive Retirement* (*PIAR*), I include portfolio income as a type of passive income, but the IRS sees it as distinct and taxes it differently. Still, portfolio income is currently taxed at no more than 20%—far less than any type of active income.

A quick recap: active income is money you earn by working, and passive income is money you earn with little to no work.

## Types of Passive Income

After much brainstorming and spreadsheeting, I am proud to define five main categories of passive income. They are (drumroll, please!):

1) Royalty Income
2) Portfolio Income
3) Coin-Operated Machines
4) Ads and E-commerce
5) Rental Income

Before we get into the how (patience, young grasshopper), I'll give you a brief overview and example of each category of passive income.

First, royalties. The first type of royalty is a payment for the use of artistic or literary works, such as copyrights, trademarks, and patents. An example of this type of royalty is Stephen King making money from his novels. Every time someone purchases one of his copyrighted books, he gets paid a royalty. Another type is a trademark, which protects brand names and logos. Think of your favorite football team. Do you own any merchandise that has that football team's logo, mascot, or name on it? When you bought that hat or shirt or jersey, the owner of that football trademark was paid a royalty. Make cents? (Pun intended.) Lastly, patents protect new inventions and designs. In 1902, when a bada$$ lady named Mary Anderson (who didn't even drive) patented the first windshield wiper, her invention was protected so that no one could copy her design, and she was able to create and sell it exclusively.[33]

The other type of royalty has to do with mineral rights. When you have mineral rights, you are entitled to mine for and produce natural resources, like oil, gas, and coal. Royalties are made when mineral rights are leased. The owner of the mineral rights gets paid by the lessee.

Portfolio income, which by the IRS is considered neither active income nor passive income, still fits the passive income definition by *my* book, since it's earned with little to no work. Portfolio income comes from interest, dividends, and investments.

With coin-operated income, you have some type of machine, and the end-user pays you for the use of that machine—think vending machines, ATMs, arcades, and laundromats.

Next, you have advertising and e-commerce. You can earn income from ads, participate in affiliate marketing, or sell products passively with dropshipping.

Rental income can be indirect or direct. You indirectly earn money from a real estate investment trust (REIT), which is covered in the portfolio income section. Or, you can directly own and lease a property, room, or storage space.

## What Passive Income *Is*

Alright, alright, alright, let's get this over with. Because I *know* some of you are thinking, "These aren't passive! It takes time to market a royalty-generating creative work; it takes time to manage tenants and fill vacancies."

By no means will I mislead or make elaborate promises about what passive income is, so: You would be correct, friend. *All* passive income streams require upfront time or capital to build in the first place, and saying that they'll magically generate cash with zero work after that would be disingenuous. But once the income stream is created and going, the work you must put in to maintain that income is minimal. Cha-ching!

Passive income has two stages: Stage 1 consists of the time, work, or money you spend *building* the income stream. Make no mistake: it's work. Stage 1 isn't the "magical" part. If you decide to create and launch a course, for example, then Stage 1 includes all the time it takes to write, edit, record, publish, market, and launch the course.

Stage 2 is when it becomes passive. After you've created, built, or launched the income stream, it's much more, if not entirely, hands-off. With a course, maybe you're putting a couple of hours in each week on marketing activities to maintain the income. Maybe you outsource even that to make it more like a couple of hours per month. Compare that to the 9-5 job where you'll be working 40 hours per week for the rest of your life. Passive income is maintained with little to no work; it's not built with little to no work. Remember how I mentioned how hard I worked for those two years building my passive income streams? I put the time in up front to get them into place, and *then* I retired.

> " *Passive income is* **maintained** *with little to no work; it's not* **built** *with little to no work.*

You may spend ten, twelve, or twenty months in Stage 1 building the passive income stream. After it's launched, in Stage 2, you put in minimal work to maintain the money coming in.

When we discuss how passive something is in this book, we are talking about *Stage 2*. We are talking about the work needed in the long run, the work needed to maintain. In other words, passivity means: once you get the thing launched, how much work must you do to maintain it?

Take rental property as another example. Rental property only becomes passive with a property manager, and even then, you still have to manage your property manager. I don't think any of us want to quit our jobs to become a full-time landlord. Sure, you can manage your properties for a few hours per month if you don't have any turnover, but to be closer to truly passive, you'll want to put a property manager in place. I'll talk about how to do that in Section Six on rental income.

Each category we will discuss is solidly in the passive income category. Instead of actively working 40 hours per week, you'll be able to put in a few hours per week or per month to maintain your passive income streams. Plus, you always have the option of outsourcing that maintenance to someone so it can be even more passive; it's up to you.

## What Passive Income *Is Not*

Passive income has nothing to do with multi-level marketing (MLM) Companies. There will be no mention of MLMs in *PIAR*. MLMs fall, without a doubt, into the active income category. It's sales, it's recruiting. Nothing about those activities are passive.

Passive income is no get-rich-quick scheme. There is no such thing. If you know of something that can magically begin generating money with no upfront time or capital investment, I'm all ears. I know we all want the easy answer, at least I do, but if I've learned anything in life, it's that nothing is free. But if it comes down to spending my time building passive income streams so that I can quickly achieve financial independence or spending my time working 40 hours per week for the rest of my life, I choose the former. And you obviously see why it can be such an exciting thing to pursue too; otherwise, you wouldn't have picked up this book!

> *Instead of actively working 40 hours per week, you'll be able to put in a few hours per week or per month to maintain your passive income streams.* „

## The Factors of SCRIMP

Repeat after me: Not all passive income is created equal. Each type has pros and cons. Luckily for you, I did my homework and created a system for evaluating one passive income stream against another using five different factors. I call them the Factors of SCRIMP.

I love that they spell out a word that means being frugal and thrifty since you *won't* have to do that once you build your passive income empire. Without further ado, here are the Factors of SCRIMP:

1) Scalability
2) Controllability & Regulation
3) Investment
4) Marketability
5) Passivity

<u>Scalability:</u> Can it be produced or offered en masse?

If you start a local cooking class, how many people can you realistically expect to sign up? Or how many people can you realistically serve? If 10,000 people show up at your front door, you'll have to turn most of them away. But what if you offered online cooking classes? Now it's a different story; you literally have no limit on the number of people that can sign up for it. *That* is the beauty of scale.

<u>Controllability & Regulation:</u> How much control do you have over it?

Let's say you start selling digital products on Etsy. All of a sudden, Etsy institutes a new policy, and you're not allowed to sell that kind of product anymore. My friend, you are SOL. That sucks. I often hear about how influencers or social-media-based businesses take a hit when Facebook or Instagram changes its algorithm. It's essential that your passive income won't be regulated by things that are outside your control.

<u>Investment:</u> What is the upfront time or capital investment in Stage 1?

Passive income is no easy money ploy. Creating passive income streams takes time or money... sometimes both. Ironic, right? You might have to spend time to free up time. Know this: you won't be able to snap your fingers and suddenly start generating $500 per month. Writing a book takes time; buying a laundromat takes money. As I list each passive income idea, I'll make it clear what the upfront investment is—whether it's months of time, hundreds or thousands of dollars, or a combination of the two. I'll also help you find ways to free up time and money so that you can get started right away.

<u>Marketability:</u> Is there a need for it?

Installing a snack vending machine in an office building that already has several snack vending machines probably won't work out too well for you. Alternatively, buying a rental property in a city that is in dire need of more rental housing likely will. Before pursuing your passive income stream, ensure it makes sense from a supply and demand perspective. Quick recap on Economics 101: If supply is greater than demand, the market is oversaturated and doesn't need any more of that item or service. If demand is greater than supply, there is a market need. Hate to break it to ya, but it doesn't matter what you're passionate about; if it's not marketable, it's not going to put food on the table.

<u>Passivity:</u> How much work must you do to maintain the income stream in Stage 2?

Buying a dividend stock and glancing at it once per year involves an entirely different level of work (or lack thereof) than operating arcade games. Some passive income streams, once up and running, will require more involvement while others will be low maintenance. Don't get me wrong; all of them are passive, but even within the passive income category, there's a sliding scale.

## A Gift from Me to You

Y'all, the original version of this book was *so long*. There's so much to know; there are so many questions I could answer! I had to cut some parts out so that I wasn't leaving you with a 400+ page book (because thanks, but no thanks). Instead, I've condensed only the top few must-know resources so that you can download them *for free*! Don't say I never did anything for ya.

Your *PIAR* Bonus Gift includes crucial (and free) supplemental info, including:

- The top three deadly mistakes to avoid when creating your passive income stream
- A simple, customizable worksheet to determine which passive income stream you should pursue first
- A time tracker activity to motivate you to get started

And much more! I recommend you download your *PIAR* Bonus Gift now at **www.moneyhoneyrachel.com/bonus** before it slips your mind. That way, you can refer to it while you're reading.

There you have it… the bones of this book. Now you know what passive income is and why it's so brilliant.

We are ready to get into the "meat" of *PIAR*! Each of the next five sections focuses on a different category of passive income. Within each category of passive income is a plethora of specific passive income ideas. As you are reading through, feel free to skip to the next chapter or section if you already know you are not interested in pursuing a certain type of passive income.

I operate from the "find a couple of things you're good at and kill it" strategy, and not the "try my hand at every single thing" strategy. Because of this mentality, and because I am only one person, I do not have personal experience with *every* passive income stream idea within *every* category of passive income. Please bear that in mind. I will speak from experience where and when I can and rely on thorough research and interviews with actual experts on the subject matter for the rest.

We will start with Royalties: The What, the Why, and the How. Here we go!

# SECTION TWO:
# Royalty Income

# CHAPTER 5

# Royalties: The What, the Why, and the How

## The What

Royalties come in all shapes and sizes, but we can categorize them into two main types. The first type of royalty is money earned by allowing others to use or view your literary or artistic work. The second type is money you make for allowing others to access minerals on your land. We'll focus on the former first.

You can earn royalties from patents, copyrights, and trademarks. You are surrounded by products that pay royalties. What music did you listen to in the car on the way to work today? Musicians make money every time their song is downloaded, and they even earn royalties from streaming services like Apple and Spotify. What have you read lately? Books, eBooks, and audiobooks are an enormous source of royalty revenue for the author. What have you worn or used lately that has a design on it? Think mugs, T-shirts, pens, phone cases and tote bags, to name a few. Artists and graphic designers can earn royalties any time a product sells that has their design on it. The possibilities are endless.

I could go on and on. Photography, software, smartphone apps, franchises, online courses, digital product sales, and basically any form of content or creative work all earn royalties.

> *s a creator, royalties are one of the most fulfilling passive income streams because you are creating something at fills a market need.*

Here's an easy way to think about it. Just ask yourself, "What can I create once, and continue to sell over and over again, forever?"

Creating a royalty-generating income stream will require an idea, creativity, and marketing. I will teach you about all these different aspects. Even if you don't feel like you fit the bill, trust me: anyone can do this! As a creator, royalties are one of the most fulfilling passive income streams because you are creating something that fills a market need.

We explore NINE types of royalties in this section. I'll explain what they are and exactly how to create each one of them. I've personally generated two of these myself and will share with you everything you need to know.

## The Why

Why are royalties an awesome type of passive income? Let's take a look at our Factors of SCRIMP.

Scalability: High. Because so many of these royalty-earning items can be sold online, it's safe to say there's a high level of scalability. You can reach hundreds of thousands of people by offering your product online.

Controllability & Regulation: Low. Think about all the ideas I've mentioned so far: music, books, photographs, designs, software, online courses, franchises, etc. Creators generally earn royalties by selling these on a platform, such as iTunes, Amazon, an App store, or Teachable. That means that you are subject to that platform's rules about how, when, and where you sell your product. The lack of control is one of the only disadvantages of royalty income.

Investment: Lots of time. *Any* artistic or creative work takes time to create. I mean, George R. R. Martin has been writing *Game of Thrones* since the '90s and *still* hasn't finished. Royalty income requires an upfront time investment more than anything. As far as dollar bills, you can invest as much money into your royalty-generating work as you want. Some will argue it absolutely requires money to launch a book or course; I disagree. I launched my first book *Money Honey* for less than $600, and I could have done it for $0 if I really wanted to. I

> **Any** artistic or creative work takes time to create.

know many people who have launched a product or service purely with their intellectual capital, not with their financial capital. You can put as little or as much money into a royalty stream as you choose.

Marketability: Depends. Is there a market for your product? You will need to research to determine if your idea has merit. One might argue that no one would be interested in purchasing a song you recorded on your xylophone because, to be blunt, no one knows who you are, and more to the point, who wants to listen to 55 minutes of the xylophone? My bet is that you'd have an extremely small market. Maybe you want to write an eBook about cryptocurrency. Great! There are literally thousands of resources out there on the topic. How will you make *your* book stand out? You can judge the market need for each product idea you come up with by doing market research. I'll show you how to do this.

Passivity: Wide range; potentially high. After Stage 1 when you create and launch your product, the amount of work to maintain the royalty income varies. Let's take this book, for example. A certain amount of marketing and social media promotion will always be necessary, even after I publish it. I'll need to ensure I am still getting my book out there, so people keep buying it, so my income stream doesn't eventually dwindle and die off. I could do this myself, working a couple of hours a week, or I could outsource the activity and pay someone else to do it. The moral of the story: If you want a truly passive stream, have a plan from the get-go to hire someone to do this ongoing work for you.

## The How

Royalty streams are such an enormous category that I'm going to take it one specific type at a time. I'll focus on the following big players when it comes to royalties.

1) Books and eBooks
2) Music
3) Photography
4) Downloadable Content
5) Print-On-Demand
6) Online courses
7) Software or app development
8) Franchising
9) Mineral Rights

I know you're eager to learn all about these nine types of royalties, and if there's one thing I know for sure about royalty-generating products, it's that you must first have a killer idea that fills a market need. Finding a marketable idea is *crucial* for success in generating this passive income stream. Therefore, it makes sense to start by learning how to come up with a bulletproof royalty-generating idea. First, you must brainstorm, and second, verify with market research.

## The Early Stages: Brainstorming

Finding a unique idea could be a potential obstacle. Why would someone buy *your* product over a different one? Think of it this way: if you're creating an online course about how to work out your lower body, how will yours be different than the thousands of gym programs already out there?

Take my idea for my royalty-generating book, *Money Honey*. The idea came to me because all my friends and family constantly asked me for financial advice, and I was able to explain things very simply to them. I had recently read the book *Skinny Bitch*, which puts a sarcastic and entertaining twist on the topic of clean eating. It was super entertaining. I thought to myself, "What if I do the same thing for personal finance?" Most other finance books are boring, dull, complicated, or intimidating. "How do I make this topic more accessible to people in my demographic?" I asked myself. And that's how the idea of creating a sassy, humorous version of a money management book came into being. That was my unique angle.

It's no easy task. My idea came to me slowly over several months. Most of the time, I wasn't even consciously thinking about it.

To create something good enough that people will want to buy it, you need to play to your strengths. If you have never touched an instrument, you probably shouldn't be selling classes on musical theory. If you lack a green thumb, writing a book about DIY gardening is probably a no-no. Get the drift?

So, your first order of business is a brainstorming sesh. Grab a pen and a couple of sheets of paper (yes, actually do it), and make a bubble chart by responding to the following questions.

What are you passionate about? You can list activities, objects, people, things—whatever. Be messy about it. The messier, the better. Don't hold back. What are your hobbies or passions? What are you really good at doing? What do people come to you for help with? What advice do people seek you out for? What activities or sports or clubs have you played or been involved in? What would your TED Talk be about? What makes you unique? What expertise do you have that others typically don't? Where have you gone that other people haven't? What have you done or achieved that other people haven't?

And then, how will you add a unique twist enabling you to offer something in the marketplace that isn't currently offered?

## Market research

Now that you have a plethora of unique ideas, it's time to verify them by conducting extensive market research. This involves finding out whether people will actually buy your work and if there is a need for it. You can start by talking to friends and family, but you must be aware of their biases. People who care about you tend to encourage and support you even if they wouldn't personally buy what you're creating. It's good to get their feedback, but take it with a grain of salt.

Use social media for market research first. Facebook groups are great places for discussion with people all over the world. You can join some groups related to your idea and ask questions or make a poll to get some feedback. This isn't about promoting yourself; it's about doing genuine research.

You can create surveys online for free and send them out to your network. I highly recommend SurveyMonkey for this. It's free to set up, and you simply email or post the link on social media asking for responses. Keep it short and simple so that people don't have to spend much time on it.

Once you get some feedback and narrow your ideas, it's time to do some research on the platform in which you will be offering your product. For books, that might be Amazon. For courses, that might be Udemy. For music, iTunes. You get the idea. I'll use launching a book on Amazon as an example, but you can recreate this research on existing platforms for any type of royalty-generating work.

Amazon has a specific ranking system that helps you research your book idea. For example, if you're thinking of writing a book about dog nutrition, you can go to Amazon's website, navigate to the books department, and type "diets for dogs" in the search bar. In this case, you would get over 2,000 results. That's your competition. There are currently over 2,000 books written on this subject available on Amazon. The first question to ask yourself is, "Can I write a top 1% book in this category?" Because that's what it will take to come up on the first two pages of the search results.

If you click on a few of the search results and open them up, you can scroll down to "Product Details" to get information about the book's sales ranking. Ranking is all that matters on Amazon, and it's an algorithm that changes hourly and is based on sales, reviews, searches, and other things that we commoners will never know. The lower number the rank, the better, with a #1 Sales Rank being the best.

I'm opening a few top results in my "diets for dogs" search. One has an overall sales rank of 406,794; one is 482,800; one is 423,212; one is 52,054. Just for perspective, I use 100,000 as a completely arbitrary number or line in the sand. I want to write stuff that resonates in such a way that it is in the top 100,000 of Amazon's books. At the time of this writing, *Money Honey* ranks 27,241.

Based on a 100,000 ranking goal, those first three search results for "diets for dogs" don't seem very promising. That last one seems out of the ordinary, so we could do some research on why that one is ranked so much better. But in general, given the rankings, this topic doesn't seem to be selling well. There could be several factors; it's too vague, or there's no demand for it, or something else entirely.

Alternately, what do the search results look like if you type in "diets for Labradors"? Your job is to continue researching Amazon until you get a good idea of what is going on within this book category. Also, does the fact that the results don't have many high-ranking book options mean that it's a non-marketable book idea or just that the existing books on this topic are poorly written? This research won't ever be black and white, so you'll have to use deductive reasoning to determine whether the demand is there and whether you can compete. For more insight into how to conduct Amazon research, I recommend this article: www.locationrebel.com/book-niches.

Not all platforms have accessible ranking systems like Amazon, but there is plenty of other information to consider:

1) The year the work was created. Are all the search results outdated? Are they all within the past few months? Why?

2) The length of any content-driven work. Are shorter or longer books, courses, or songs in this category selling better?

3) Again, the number of search results in your category. If your search only returns eighty results, you will have less competition versus a search that returns 10,000+ results.

4) The reviews. What makes this work good and another work bad? Why do people like or dislike this work? Are people complaining about the same thing over and over, and if so, does that mean there is a need that is unfulfilled? Can you fill that need?

5) The price. Is your competition priced over $100? Under $10? Do you see any patterns? How much could you reasonably price your work compared to the others?

You could spend hours on this, and I encourage you to. *Your* time and *your* money are on the line, and you must ensure there is a demand for what you are creating and that you understand exactly what you are up against.

Next, we'll discuss how each type of royalty works, how passive it is, and how you can begin with specific actions and steps, starting with books and eBooks.

# CHAPTER 6

# Introducing Books and eBooks

Each time someone buys a book you have published, you are paid a portion of the revenue via royalties.

For example, every time someone buys *Twilight*, which has a retail price of $22.99 for the hardcover version, Stephenie Meyer is paid a percentage of that revenue as a royalty. Neither you nor I have any idea how much she makes per book since that all depends on her agreement with her publisher.

Just for fun, let's say Stephenie makes $2.00 per hardcover, which is about 9%. If she sells ten hardcovers per month, she'd earn $20 per month. One hundred books sold would be $200 per month. One thousand books would be $2,000 per month. You get the picture. Stephenie doesn't just have a hardcover version of *Twilight*, though. She has a paperback, eBook, and audiobook. Depending on sales volume and the royalty percentage, you can see how it would be possible for a well-known author to make $10,000 or $20,000 per month from this income stream. Yes, yes, that figure would likely take a major bestseller, but think about writing a much more moderately-successful book and making $1,500 per month. And then cloning that process and writing another. All it would take is a handful of books to make a pretty hefty passive income stream.

## My Experience

My $10,000+ per month in passive income currently consists of three things: my rental income, my book royalties, and my print-on-demand royalties.

*Passive Income, Aggressive Retirement (PIAR)* is my second book. My first book, *Money Honey: A Simple 7-Step Guide for Getting Your Financial $hit Together*, was and is a huge hit. It's been on Amazon's Finance Bestsellers List multiple times, has over 400 five-star reviews, and has been downloaded and sold over 10,000 times.

When I began writing *Money Honey*, I never incorporated it into my passive income stream plan and goals. It was a passion project. The only reason I even went through with publishing that book is because I believed that if I could help just one person, it would be worth it. It was never about the money, and I never put a dollar figure goal to it because I didn't want to get my hopes up.

Nevertheless, it now brings in a substantial amount of money, and I have been lucky to monetize something that I am passionate about, and that helps people. My advice is, if you go this route, to have some sense of motivation other than just the money.

## Stages 1 and 2

The actual writing of a book occurs in Stage 1 when you build the passive income stream. This particular royalty stream mostly requires an upfront time investment. It could take months to write, publish, and launch your book. You can invest money into it too, if you want. Many people choose to invest thousands of dollars into their book launch and marketing. I opted to keep costs as low as possible with *Money Honey*. My initial costs were under $600, and half of that was paid to my book editor. I could have spent much less if I had decided to. Regardless of how much money you invest in Stage 1, there's no getting around that initial time investment.

After you launch the book and get it going, the time you spend sustaining it in Stage 2 is completely up to you. Stage 2 is where you make your passive income. If you want to make it 100% passive, then you can, by outsourcing marketing activities. However, there are some things only the author can do, so if you don't want to miss out on those things, then you could also make it 90% passive and spend a couple of hours per week making appearances, doing interviews, and being on podcasts. The cool thing is, you get to design any long-term marketing efforts based on what you want. Book royalties definitely can be on the "more passive" side of the passive income scale.

> *I opted to keep costs as low as possible with* Money Honey. *My initial c* *under $* **"**

We discussed in the previous chapter the importance of brainstorming and conducting market research when it comes to creating a royalty-generating stream of passive income. For books and eBooks, the next step is outlining and writing it.

## Outlining and Writing

Once you have verified your book idea with market research, you gotta write thing. Easier said than done. For nonfiction, which is what I have experience writing, I think it's best to go with the outlining technique. I don't have personal experience with fiction but from the research I've done, techniques differ by author. Some people are Team Plotter and some are Team Pantser. Plotters like to outline and Pantsers like to make it up as they go.

By the way, if you don't think you're a strong writer, don't let that stop you. Lack of confidence is a potential fallback for many, but you can always enlist a trusted contact to act as your ghostwriter or hire a professional ghostwriter to turn your thoughts and ideas into a cohesive book.

If you choose to write it yourself, I think outlining makes the writing process easier. Start by thinking about how you would naturally divide up your book into a few large sections. Then brainstorm sub-sections. It doesn't have to be organized. You can do a bulleted list, a mind map, or just write words and phrases. Get as many general ideas for your book as possible on paper.

Finally, you'll take that paper and translate it into a cohesive outline. Where should your book naturally start? Which section should go first, and which should go last? Work on transforming your ideas into an order that makes sense. Once you do this, you should have a pretty good structure for your book.

Before writing, you can make one more attempt at broadening your outline by going in and adding further supporting details and bullets. The more you fill it in, the easier it will be to write because you already know exactly what comes next.

The writing flow will come and go. Sometimes, you will sit down and feel like you could write all night long, and you really get in the groove. Other times, you'll sit down, stare at the page, write two words in twenty minutes, and yell at the wall. The trick is to not be too hard on yourself. Just be consistent. With *Money Honey,* at first, I was excited to get started. Words poured out of me. But over time, it was less fun, and I felt like I was running out of things to say. Writer's block is real, y'all. Do not worry. You will get there, as long as you are consistent. Get in a good schedule where you are setting time aside daily—even if it's only ten minutes.

Once you have a first draft, take a little break from it. Give yourself one to two weeks off so that your brain can disengage. Giving yourself time off will allow you to look at your manuscript with a fresh set of eyes.

After a couple weeks, come back for your first edit. Print a hard copy, read through the whole thing, and take notes with a pen. Think about things like the flow, transitions, and structure. Is anything redundant? What could you cut out to make the book better? What needs more clarification?

These notes and revisions will get you to your second draft, at which point I recommend picking two or three close, well-read, grammatically knowledgeable friends or family members to do another round of editing, so your book is in the best shape possible.

Et voilà. You now know how to outline and write your book. Before we get into the next step, which entails determining the best way to publish your book, we're going to hear from Honorée Corder, who has written dozens of books and built a business around helping others do the same.

## A Case Study: Honorée Corder, Author and Executive Book Coach

I'm bursting with excitement to introduce Honorée Corder. Honorée is an executive book coach, TEDx speaker, and author of dozens of books. Get this: she partnered with the self-help guru Hal Elrod to expand his *Miracle Morning*™ series. Pretty sweet, right? Honorée helps people develop multiple streams of income through book writing and publishing. She even has a coaching course called *You Must Write a Book*, and her bada$$ery is legendary. I had the opportunity to pick her brain about royalties and passive income. Check it out:

Me: *Take us all the way back to Day One. Why did you write your first book?*

Honorée: *I wrote the book because I saw Mark Victor Hansen, the co-creator of the* Chicken Soup for the Soul Series, *speak at an event. Afterward, he asked me what I did, and I said, "I am a coach and a speaker," and he said, "Everyone is a coach and a speaker. You must write a book." Mark asked me, "Do you have a speech that you've given over and over again that people like?" And I said, "Yes." And he said, "That's your first book." That was in 2004.*

At that time, Honorée had already been a business coach for many years. But the book she was about to write was what differentiated her and ultimately allowed her to charge more for her speaking, training, and coaching.

Me: *How long did it take you to write from start to finish?*

Honorée: *I sat in a chair—I have tremendous endurance—and I typed the speech, which runs an hour, but it took me 40 hours to write because I was putting in examples and references.*

*My first book is what is now the 10ᵗʰ-anniversary edition of* Tall Order! *The very first edition of that book is going to remain nameless; it's the book that I made all the mistakes with, it had a terrible title and terrible cover, and I didn't do any editing on it. All the things I teach now? I did not know to do them.*

Honorée strategically designed the book to fit into a gentleman's breast pocket of his suit jacket. When she was networking, and people asked for a business card, she would give them her book. "The WOW factor was very high," she says.

Honorée published the book and ordered five thousand copies from the printer (back then, there were no print-on-demand platforms or eBooks). While the book was at the printer, she sold eleven thousand copies!

Honorée: *In those first three weeks, I did what Mark Victor Hansen told me to do. He said, "Do seven things to market your book every day." At the time, it was things like contact your local newspaper, contact your local TV station, try to get in local magazines. I called everyone in my Rolodex, and I asked them what Mark told me to ask, which was, "Would you like to buy between ten and one thousand copies of the book?" He actually told me to ask for between ten and one hundred copies, except I was a business coach, and my clients were CEOs, COOs, CMOs. I knew they had a larger purchasing ability. Some of them had sales teams with one to three thousand people. So, I sold books in blocks. The smallest orders I would take were five, ten, or fifteen books. I just had an order form that I had created in Microsoft Word. I would email it to people, and they'd print it out, fill it out, and send it to me with a check.*

*I wasn't doing anything exciting or sexy. I was Dialing for Dollars; I was just going through and making the ask. That's where I started. With that original book, I sold eleven thousand copies in three weeks.*

Although she *sold* her books in smaller blocks, Honorée *ordered* her books in blocks of five thousand. They cost 80 cents a book to print. So, she would order five thousand copies for $4,000. That meant she could also give away a lot of books and still make a nice profit. There were no other costs at the time for launching her book.

Me: *Did you know right away that you wanted to self-publish?*

Honorée: *I'm a farm girl from Ohio. I never went to college, I never took* t *consider myself a capital 'W' writer. It never even occurred to me to figure out the path for traditional publishing.*

> I'm a farm girl from Ohio. I never went to college, I never took a writing class, and I did not consider myself a capital 'W' writer.
>
> -Honorée Corder

*In my mind, someone who got a traditional book deal was someone who had a college degree and who would then be worthy and deserving of a traditional book deal. Now, my thought process is completely different.*

When Honorée launched her first book, she didn't realize how big this business would become. Her first book set things in motion; she got a weekly spot on TV in Las Vegas, and she was busy for a few years. Then, five years after her first book, life *really* changed.

Honorée: *I was watching an Oprah show in 2009 where they were doing a makeover. I had been a single mom for several years, and one of the women was a single mom, and that makeover inspired me to write* The Successful Single Mom *book, which is now a six-book series. I kind of got the fever, but it was delayed.*

Today, Honorée is the author of more than fifty books. She helps people write, publish, and market their books and turn them into multiple streams of six-figure income. She even has a course called the *You Must Write a Book Live Coaching Course*, and she has the Empire Builder's Mastermind, which is an exclusive group for people who want to build a seven-figure empire with at least one of their income streams from a book.

Me: *Is royalty income truly passive, or can it be truly passive?*

Honorée: *I think book royalties are passive income by the loose definition but not by the strict definition. I have my Y Must Write a Book Live Coach Course, and in that course teach that there are two pha of a book's life. Phase One beg the minute you conceive of book idea until about thirty d after your launch. Phase 1 starts after your launch, an ends when you die. I set expectation that there is a re long marketing tail marketing the book. If you d feed the beast, the beast will die.*

> " *me to, as a single mom, support my daughter. I know... in 2020... I'm going to make hundreds of thousands of dollars from my royalty income... and that has given me a certain sense of security.*
>
> -Honorée Corder

Me: *What about if you hire someone to market it for you, then is it passive?*

Honorée: *There are marketing activities that can be done in absentia, like someone can write and manage ads and those sorts of things. But just like when Julia Roberts stars in a new movie, she can't hire someone to go to* The Today Show *and talk about her new film. People want to hear from the creator.*

Me: *What has royalty income been able to do for you? How has it changed your life?*

Honorée: *It allowed me to, as a single mom, support my daughter and to have a very nice lifestyle. Having that royalty income has given me the financial freedom to do other things that I wanted to do. I'm not locked into something. I get to pursue things that I'm excited about because I have royalty income coming in. I know I'm going to wake up, and in 2020 I'm going to make hundreds of thousands of dollars from my royalty income from my books before the year has even started, and that has given me a certain sense of security. I don't say that to be braggadocious or obnoxious, but if it's possible for me, and if I can do it—see my previous comments about no education—then it is possible for anyone to do that as long as they are willing to do the work, and that's the asterisk. You're going to have to work smart and hard, and you're going to have to keep working. There is no "one-and-done." If you recognize that, then awesome, because the alternative is a 9-5, and guess what? That's not passive at any stage of the game.*

> *5, and guess what? That's not passive at any stage of the game.*

Honorée is #goals. You can check out her website at www.honoreecorder.com. Grab a copy of *You Must Write a Book* if you're interested in pursuing this passive income stream. Give Honorée a follow on social media, too!

Facebook: www.facebook.com/Honoree

Instagram: www.instagram.com/honoree

Twitter: www.twitter.com/Honoree

Now that you know how royalties from books work and how to outline and write your book, we're ready to dive into the details of publishing. Up next, I'll explain everything you need to know to when it comes to deciding whether to self-publish or traditionally publish.

# CHAPTER 7

# *The Great Debate on Publishing*

## **P**ublishing Options

Let's go ahead and end the Great Debate. Should you find a traditional publisher, or should you self-publish?

When you find a traditional publisher, you are selling the rights to the manuscript to a book publishing company. In turn, the publisher sets you up with an editor to help you revise and write the best version of your book possible so that it will be appealing to a broader audience. One possible downside is that the publisher gets the final say on everything, from content to book cover. Another hurdle is that to be published by a reputable house, a writer typically needs an agent to represent them and negotiate the deal. The agent, in return, gets paid a percentage of revenue from the book sales. As you can imagine, finding a reputable agent to get your book on the desk of an editor at a good house is a feat.

Working with a publisher means giving up most of your revenue. Earning an 8% to 15% royalty is pretty typical when you publish traditionally. If your paperback is priced at $15.00, you might only make $1.50 on each sale.

Contrary to popular belief, you are still responsible for most, if not all, of the marketing and promotion of your book, even when you get a publishing deal. Your publisher almost certainly won't send you on a book tour. In fact, it's hard to land a traditional publishing deal if you don't have a significant following or platform. Why? Because the publisher expects you to be able to sell the book yourself to an already-existing audience.

Once you have a publishing agreement in place, you'll be paid. The publisher pays an agreed-upon advance, which is an amount of money paid to the author up front, sometimes before the author is even finished with the book. This is a benefit for authors who are relying on the income. Essentially, it's an advance of royalties from sales; the author is being paid part of the royalties up front. Then, after the book is published, the author gets a percentage of the royalties, but only after the advance is paid back in full. For example, if the author is paid a $20,000 advance, then she won't receive any payment for the initial sales until the sales have generated $20,000 in royalties. The author will only be paid royalties once she surpasses the first $20,000. This puts the risk of the success of the book launch on the publisher, who would be out $20,000 from the very beginning in a calculated bet that they'd be able to recompense at least the amount of money invested in you, the writer. The publisher only gets its investment back if the book does well.

When you self-publish, you are essentially doing all of this on your own and taking on all the risk. You write, edit, revise, design, format, and publish the book yourself. You market and promote the book on your own, which you'd be expected to do anyway if you traditionally published. You pay for printing, decide your price, and (the best part) get to keep a much larger percentage of the royalties. If you self-publish on Amazon, you are paid anywhere from 35% to 70% of the revenue. There is no requirement for having a platform or following or being already established as a writer. And, you have complete creative control over your work.

Which option works for you? I'll highlight the biggest factors to consider:

1) Time: Finding a traditional publisher is difficult and time-consuming; conversely, nothing is stopping you from self-publishing a book today.

2) Money and Risk: With a traditional publisher, you are responsible for completing the manuscript and helping to market and promote the book. The publisher foots the bill for all the costs: cover art, editing, printing, and advertising. The publisher takes on the risk, and in return, you are paid a small percentage of the revenue. If you self-publish, you pay for everything and take on the risk, and you get to keep much more of the revenue.

3) Control: A traditional publisher gets the final say on every aspect of your book. On the other hand, self-publishing means you are fully in control of your book.

Those are the three main differences between traditional and self-publishing. Either option, if successful, will result in passive income.

## How-To: Traditional Publishing

If you opt for the traditional publishing route, your goal is to find a publisher. After that, you will work with the publisher to make changes and launch the book.

Writing: First, write the thing. Easy! (JK, maybe not that easy.) After you brainstorm your ideas, it's about putting pen to paper. I highly recommend starting with an outline to get your creative juices flowing, especially if your book is nonfiction.

Finding an agent: You'll need to work with a literary agent to get your work in front of a well-known publisher. Think of an agent like you would a realtor or broker—someone who matches up potential buyers and sellers to facilitate business. A literary agent does this for authors and publishers. You'll start by researching agents. You can use sites like WritersMarket.com or AgentQuery.com. Create a massive list of all possible agents and narrow it down from there, based on their experience and who works with your genre. You'll send your submission to the agent, they will send it off to a publisher, and if the publisher is interested, the agent will negotiate a deal for you.

<u>Preparing your submission:</u> Every agent and publisher has different requirements for how to submit your work, but these are the most common items you'll be asked to prepare:

- Query letter: Think of this as a one-page description (a sales pitch, really) on why the publisher should consider your work. It's a cover letter for your book. You can easily Google examples for ideas of how to structure and write this. Often, your initial submission will consist of sending query letters to dozens of agents, who may then ask you for more information.

- Novel synopsis: A novel synopsis is a brief book summary for a fiction book. It's normally one to two pages in length and includes the book ending.

- Nonfiction book proposal: A nonfiction book proposal is like a business plan for your book. You should articulate to the publisher why there is a need for the book and sell them on the idea. A book proposal is normally much longer than a novel synopsis.

- Sample chapters or manuscript: Fiction tends to be submitted to the publisher as a completed manuscript. You'll want to provide the best manuscript you possibly can. Do not rush. Nonfiction can be submitted with a few sample chapters starting at the beginning of the book.

These items are not always needed right away. You might start off by simply submitting a query letter to the agent, and then the agent might ask you for more in order to submit to a publisher.

And that, folks, is the quick and dirty of how to pursue traditional publishing.

## How-To: Self-Publishing

Reading *Published* by Chandler Bolt inspired me to put pen to paper with *Money Honey*. It taught me 99% of what I needed to know to self-publish. Bolt's guide is completely comprehensive and covers every step of the process, from brainstorming to outlining to writing to marketing to launching. I'll explain my own, specific process regarding marketing and launching best practices (see Chapter 12), but I highly recommend using *Published* as an extensive guide for how to self-publish a book.

The decision to self-publish *Money Honey* and *PIAR* was a no-brainer. All the marketing I did for *Money Honey*, I would have had to do with a traditional publisher anyway, so why give up most of my royalty? It's no secret that I'm biased—I've only ever self-published—but I do think it's the way to go for first-time authors.

It's not always one or the other. One of the best parts about self-publishing is that, should your book be a success, a publishing house can always pick you up later! So really, there's little downside when it comes to self-publishing, as long as you're willing to put in the work to market yourself and build a following on the front end.

When you traditionally publish, the publisher takes care of all the deets. But when you self-publish, you're responsible for everything and anything. The three most important aspects of getting your book ready are editing, cover design, and formatting.

Edit your book: After finalizing the second draft of your book, you will decide whether to pay for a professional edit. For the record, a good editor is worth his or her weight in gold. I highly recommend using Upwork or Fiverr to find an editor at a reasonable price. I paid $250 for a Fiverr editor for *Money Honey*, which is thousands less than a standard market rate.

Design your cover: Another item on your plate will be coming up with a book cover design. This, too, can be outsourced, or you can create your own depending on your time and budget constraints. If you opt to DIY, you can use Canva or take some Photoshop tutorials. I created the cover of *Money Honey* by myself in Photoshop, but for *PIAR*, I paid a professional on 99designs.com.

Format your book: Lastly, you'll need to format your book to get it ready for publishing. I self-publish using Amazon's platform, Kindle Direct Publishing (KDP). KDP has options for publishing both an eBook and a paperback version. Because of the overwhelming popularity of Amazon, this will likely be your best chance to get your book in front of the most people possible if you are self-publishing, but you can also explore the other platforms like IngramSpark, Lulu, Apple Books, and Kobo. You can either hire someone to format your book, or you can research the platform's requirements and do it yourself to save some money.

Next up, we'll hear from one of the most successful self-publishing stories in existence: Hal Elrod.

## A Case Study: Hal Elrod, International Bestselling Author & Keynote Speaker

Ladies and gents, are you in for a treat! It is a complete honor and privilege to introduce you to the internationally bestselling author of *The Miracle Morning*™ Series, Hal Elrod! Hal is one of the most extraordinary people I know, and you'll agree once you hear his story.

When he was just twenty years old, Hal died when a drunk driver hit his car head-on. His heart stopped for six minutes. He eventually woke up from a coma to be told by doctors that he probably would never walk again. Get this: not only did Hal walk, but he also went on to run a 52-mile ultra-marathon! At age 26, Hal then wrote and self-published his first book, *Taking Life Head On*.

After several years of achievement, Hal was slammed by the 2008 Recession. He found himself in over $425,000 of debt and struggling with severe depression. To fight his way out, he committed to focusing on personal growth and created a morning routine to help him do so. It worked wonders for him, so he shared it with his coaching clients. Once he realized how special his *Miracle Morning* was, he knew it was his obligation to share it with the public.

> "
> *pursue traditional publishing... But throughout the process of writing the book and researching the difference... I came to the conclusion, 'Wait. I'd be 1etter off to self-publish*
>
> -Hal Elr(

*The Miracle Morning* (*TMM*) went on to become one of the most successful self-publishing achievements *in the world*. *TMM* has been translated into 37 languages, has over 3,000 five-star reviews, and has impacted the lives of over *two million people* in over seventy countries.

Hal is the host of the *Achieve Your Goals* podcast, a hall of fame business achiever, an international keynote speaker, and, most importantly, a grateful husband and father.

I was truly blessed to pick Hal's brain on self-publishing vs. traditional publishing and how passive income has changed his life.

Me: *Why did you decide to self-publish The Miracle Morning?*

Hal: *Originally, I was going to pursue traditional publishing because back in 2009, when I was writing the book, self-publishing was not really respected, or at least that was my perception. I originally hired a gal to help me write a [book] proposal. She had helped another famous author get a million-dollar book advance, so I thought, "I'll hire her, I want the best." She helped me put together a thirty-page book proposal for publishers. But throughout the process of writing the book and researching the difference between self and traditional publishing, I came to the conclusion, "Wait. I'd be better off to self-publish."*

Me: *Why? What are the biggest benefits of self-publishing over traditional publishing?*

Hal: *I recommend self-publishing for 99% of new authors. Here's the deal—the publisher doesn't base your advance on how good your [book] idea is. They only base it on the size of your platform. **That is it**. The only reason to pursue traditional publishing is if you have a significant platform. A platform is a group of people that know you, like you, trust you, with whom you have a direct line of communication. I say you need a hundred thousand people you can reach through email lists, social media—maybe you can say ten thousand, minimum, is when you can start even considering it.*

*Here's another reason self-publishing trumps traditional. Instead of getting an average of 12% per book [in royalties], you usually get 70% per book.*

*Lastly, [a traditional publisher] has creative control. If you wanted to do spinoffs, turn it into a series, [the publisher] would have owned that. If you do traditional, you want to really read the contract and ask yourself, "What might I want to do in the future? Might I want to write a second* book that's a spinoff? Might I want to do an event based on this or create an online course based on the content of the book?" [Traditional publishers] own you. They own the rights to everything that you could ever do with that book.

Hal self-published *TMM* in 2012, and it slowly but surely took off. Two years later, after he had sold 100,000 copies and built a significant platform, Hal once again considered traditional publishing. He found an agent and began pitching to publishers.

Hal: *We met with 13 publishers, and we got nine offers on the original book, and the top two offers were for $250,000 advances. With how much money I was earning [self-publishing] at the time, none of those advances made sense financially.*

> *We met with 13 publishers… and the top two offers were for $250,000 advances. With how much money I was earning [self-publishing] at the time, none of those advances nade sense financially.*
>
> -Hal Elrod

But one publisher brought up a fascinating idea to Hal: keep his self-published rights in the US, and sign deals with foreign rights publishers. This specific utilization of traditional publishing has been enormously beneficial; *TMM* has now been translated into 37 languages.

Hal: *The income from foreign royalties matches, maybe even this year will surpass, the US. I mean, it's crazy. There are 37 streams of income from all these different publishers. And checks just show up! Like yesterday I got two checks in the mail: one was for $4,000 and change, one for $11,000 and change. They just show up every week or two. So, you could actually be self-published and traditionally published.*

To date, Hal has written over ten books. His latest was *The Miracle Equation*, which was released in 2019. But, plot twist: he went with traditional publishing for the first time ever.

Me: *At that point with* The Miracle Equation, *why did you make the switch?*

Hal: *There are a few different reasons. I wrote a book, which I have yet to publish, called* Beyond the Bestseller: How to Write a Book that Creates Movement, Earns You a Fortune, and Changes the World. *In that book, I make the case of why I believe authors should pursue self-publishing. But I felt unqualified to fully give the advice because my only experience was that I had turned down nine traditional publishers for* The Miracle Morning. *Yes, I've done it in foreign markets but not in the US. To me, I was missing that piece. So, that was one reason; I wanted to try it out for the knowledge and the experience and the credibility. I wanted to publish traditionally to compare the two.*

*Another reason was that, to be very transparent, I had established credibility as an author, and I had the platform (in terms of the amount of people I can reach). So, I had the leverage to negotiate a very lucrative publishing deal. It made the risk worth it. So* ˮ I'm allowed to say this—the advance was $800,000 for* The Miracle Equation.

*But here's the deal.* The Miracle Morning *has earned close to $4 million as a self-published book, but you don't get an advance. So that's where that $800,000 seems like a lot of money, but not when I look at what I'm risking, losing millions and millions of dollars.*

> " *had the leverage to negotiate a very lucrative publishing deal... the advance was $800,000 for* The Miracle Equation. "
>
> -Hal Elrod

*It's funny, my dream for* The Miracle Morning *when I was writing it—I wrote a check for $100,000 from a New York publisher to myself. Like, I printed a blank check off the internet, and I just put it on my vision board. And if that dream [of getting a traditional book deal] would've come true, I would have missed out on the biggest financial opportunity that my family has ever had.*

Me: *How many copies are you selling per month of* The Miracle Morning *now, and how much income does that generate?*

Hal: *We average ten thousand copies a month in the United States, and earn, let's say conservatively, $6 per book in self-published royalties. And that does not include our foreign sales. In international sales, we are* *selling more. In Brazil alone, we've sold over 500,000 copies this year. We're selling more in Brazil than in the United States. That's one country. And it's in 37.*

Readers, I did the math for ya. In the United States alone, *TMM* is generating approximately $720,000 in passive, royalty income per year!

Me: *What's the one thing you did in your business and your book that allowed you to succeed?*

Hal: *Most books don't change behavior. If somebody reads a book and gets great ideas, they might talk about the book while they're reading it, but as soon as they're done reading it, they move onto the next book, and that's the book they're talking about.*

*The Miracle Morning centers around doing these six practices to enhance your life radically—the S.A.V.E.R.S.—and it culminates in a thirty-day challenge where I hold their hand because most people struggle with self-discipline.*

*to writing a book that changes the world is to teach people how to change their behavior in a meaningful way.*

*The number-one key to writing a book that changes the world is to teach people how to change their behavior in a meaningful way. The entire book needs to culminate into simple, step-by-step behavior change.*

*Whether it's six months or six years later, if they're still doing the thing that you taught them in your book, if you're still adding value to their life, they're still going to be talking about your book.* With The Miracle Morning, *I have people tell me to this day they've been doing it for seven years now. They've done thousands of* Miracle Mornings.

Hal's royalty income has been extremely passive for years, but it took him time to build up to that point. *TMM* was not an overnight success. Hal spent 18 months doing excessive promotion, including podcast interviews, speeches, and talk shows, before he even sold two thousand copies per month. But after Stage 1, once he got it off the ground, it became very passive.

Me: *In terms of royalty income in general and the income you generate from your books, how passive do you think it is?*

Hal: *I would say it's approximately 95% passive. Here's why. In 2016, I sold 131,000 copies of* The Miracle Morning. *I did over seventy podcast interviews on other people's podcasts, I did 52 of my own podcast interviews to keep getting the word out, I gave 36 speeches, I ran a live event, I was on a few television shows. And all of that led to me selling 131,000 copies.*

*On October 28, 2016, I was diagnosed with a rare, aggressive form of cancer and given a 20 to 30% chance of survival.*

*In 2017, I spent most of my time fighting for my life at the hospital, battling this cancer with aggressive chemotherapy. I gave zero podcast interviews. I ran zero episodes of my own podcast. I did give four speeches. I did zero televisi*c *interviews. And I couldn't go my event. And I sold 130,0*0 *copies. I was a thousand copi short of the year before. I r*c *zero ads either year. It was* c *word of mouth.*

Me: *Wow. That is powerf*u *What has royalty income do*n *for you? How has it chang*e *your life?*

Hal: *When I had cancer, allowed me to focus on* m *healing. Beyond that, passi*n *income has allowed me to ha*v *the freedom to live life on* m *terms—freedom to do wh*i *matters most to me. And that focus on my health, spend time with my family, make an impact in the world, and not have to make any of those decisions based on money.*

> **Passive income has allowed me to have... freedom to do what matters most to me. And that is focus on my health, spend time with my family, make an impact in the world, and not have to make any of those decisions based on money.**
>
> -Hal Elrod

You can check out Hal's website at HalElrod.com. Make sure to pick up a copy of his book *The Miracle Morning*—I can personally attest to how life-changing it is. Don't forget to follow Hal on social media.

Facebook: www.facebook.com/yopalhal

Instagram: www.instagram.com/hal_elrod

Twitter: www.twitter.com/HalElrod

That's a wrap for books and eBooks, the first type of royalty income. You might have noticed that I have not yet discussed launching and marketing strategies... The reality is that launching and marketing your royalty-generating product is similar for each type of royalty income. Rather than bore you with the details over and over again, I hit on launching and marketing for *all types of royalty income* at the end of the section in Chapter 12.

On deck, we have another type of royalty income: Music.

# CHAPTER 8

# Do-Re-Mi-Fa-So-La-Ti-Do

**The What & The Why**

Give it up for music royalties!

Earning money as a successful musician is not as simple as writing a song, recording it, and selling it to earn money from your sales. If you're interested in making passive income from your music, it's vital that you understand what kind of royalty streams are out there. Anyone involved in the creation of music can earn royalties three primary ways:

1) Mechanical Royalties: Money earned from CDs, streaming, and downloads.

2) Public Performance Royalties: Money earned when the music is played publicly on the radio, on TV, at a club, etc.

3) Synchronization Royalties: Money earned when the music is paired with visual media, as in commercials, video games, ads, etc.

There are two types of music copyrights: master rights and publishing rights. If you were reallll confused about my girl Taylor Swift's feud regarding owning her masters, listen up. A master recording is the original recorded version of the song. Master rights usually belong to the artist, record label, or recording studio. In Taylor's case, they belonged to her record label company that was sold, something she had no control over.

Publishing rights, on the other hand, belong to the owner of the actual musical composition—the notes, melodies, rhythms, and lyrics, for example. Clear as mud, right?

Because there are so many different players involved in music creation, and because copyright is an intricate knot of rules, and because streaming platforms have watered down profits, it's difficult to make money from music. There's a shocking amount of leakage through the whole music business.

Like publishing a book, selling your music will require an initial investment of time and possibly even money. Putting the work in during Stage 1 is essential. Dropping a song takes a ton of work.

Is this really passive in the long run (AKA Stage 2)? Whatever path you pursue as a musician will impact the passivity, but one might argue that royalties from music are less passive than some of the other ideas in this book. Maybe if you're a songwriter and pull off a couple of billboard hits, you can stop working for the rest of your life. How passive a royalty income stream is depends on how much success you have.

## The How

An artist must register with a Performing Rights Organization (PRO) to get paid many of the different royalties. The three PROs in the US are ASCAP, BMI, and SESAC. Each has different requirements, membership fees, and benefits of joining.

These days, recording a song generally involves recording each instrument separately and combining them later (as opposed to earlier days of recording entire performances in single takes.) This multitrack recording allows artists to shape the sound of each instrument and have more control over the final product. To be physically able to do this, you'll need some equipment: software and a microphone at a minimum.

Multitrack recording starts with creating a track, which keeps the tempo for the other instruments. Then you record the rhythm, normally with drums or bass; the harmonies, with guitar, piano, horns, etc.; and the melodies, usually with lead vocals. Next, you edit, mix, and master your song. Any of these steps can be done on your own or outsourced to an expert. At the risk of sounding like a broken record (hehe), Fiverr and Upwork are great resources.

Once you have a master, it's time to publish your music. Exactly like with publishing a book, you can find a publisher or self-publish, and the pros and cons are very similar. When you find a publisher, they take a percentage of the royalties in exchange for handling copyright, promotion, and PRO registration. When you self-publish, you do this on your own and make more money.

Since I don't personally have experience with creating music royalties, I turned to two seriously impressive musicians: music veteran Thom Shepherd and newcomer Landon Sears. These guys answered all of my questions on how this income stream works and how passive it really is.

## A Case Study: Thom Shepherd, CMA of Texas Songwriter of the Year

CMA of Texas Songwriter of the Year Thom Shepherd got his first publishing deal in 1998. He has been touring in Texas with his wife since 2011, so he's had over twenty years of experience in the industry. When he creates a song, he handles every aspect, from writing to producing to launching to performing.

Thom's first hit song was "Riding with Private Malone" back in 2001. One song was all it took for Thom to reach the point at which he was making enough money from his music to live comfortably. You can find his music everywhere: iTunes, Spotify, Google Play, Pandora, Napster, Apple Music, and more. During our conversation, Thom explained how the shift towards streaming and downloads has really hurt the music industry.

Me: *What are the pros and cons of the different platforms on which you offer your music?*

Thom: *You used to sell a $15 CD, and everyone got paid, and it didn't matter if you had a hit song or not because people had to buy the whole thing. Downloads affected business quite a bit because people only bought the singles and the ones on the radio and not so much the other songs on the record.*

*All the streaming services pay a different amount, anywhere from .001 cents to .003 cents to .006 cents. Napster merged with Rhapsody, and they are one of the highest paying ones now. They pay .016 cents per stream. But that might be the whole piece that's paid out, so I only get a part of that. The pie is sometimes cut two or four ways when you account for the publisher or co-writer.*

> **[Songwriting] is a lifetime kind of thing. It goes beyond your life actually... after you die, your family gets the royalties for another 75 years.** "
>
> -Thom Shepherd

Me: *As a songwriter, how much work do you do in the long run? What does it take to sustain the income stream?*

Thom: *It's not really the songwriter's job to market it or sustain it. If you're just the songwriter, it has its own life, and it's out of your hands. If you're both the songwriter and performer, all songs have a lifespan. You put it out as a single to the radio, you work it and try to get it up the chart, and when it peaks and goes as far as it's gonna go, then you kinda move onto the next one. You definitely have to keep creating music to keep making money. If you want to have a long-term career and people to keep coming back, you always have to be coming up with something new.*

Thom explains that songwriting is the most passive aspect of creating music. When someone records it, the songwriter gets paid for life on it.

Thom: *You know "Drift Away" by Dobie Gray? The guy that wrote that is Mentor Williams, and he licensed that song hundreds of times. Tons of people have recorded it. Not just the people that had the hit with it, but by people you've never heard of, and all those folks have to pay him. It's a lifetime kind of thing. It goes beyond your life actually—life plus 75 years— after you die, your family gets the royalties for another 75 years.*

Me: *Would you recommend that others try to pursue this avenue as a passive income stream?*

Thom: *I think it's one of those things that if you have a passion for doing it, do it, but would I recommend it as a job to somebody to make a living? Not really. It's very competitive. It's tough to make that hit song kind of money. It has to be your passion or what you love doing.*

> *that hit song kind of money. It has to be your passion or what you love doing.*
>
> -Thom Shepherd

Me: *What else would you want readers of my book to know?*

Thom: *There's a songwriter, Jim McBride, in Nashville. When people ask him, "Should I move to Nashville and pursue songwriting?" his answer is, "I wouldn't move there unless I felt like I was gonna die if I didn't. If you're any less passionate than that, don't move there." I think he's right. I love doing what we do; we tour and travel. When someone asks me, "What do you like best, writing a song or performing one live?" My answer is always, "Performing a song I wrote, live."*

A round of applause for Thom! Better yet, check out his website for his most current music and news at www.thomshepherd.com. You can also follow him on social media:

Facebook: www.facebook.com/ThomShepherdmusic

Instagram: www.instagram.com/thomshepherd

Twitter: www.twitter.com/THOMSHEPHERD

## A Case Study: Landon Sears, Nashville Musician

Next, we have Landon Sears. Landon is an R&B, Soul, Hip Hop artist in Nashville. His first and best instrument is the violin, which he began playing at age seven. He also plays guitar, sings, and raps. Sears began releasing music in 2014, launched his first album in 2017, and has thousands of listeners from all over the US. His music is fresh and original; before you read further, put on his song "Blueberry Cadillac."

In terms of creating his music, Landon does everything. He produces it, mixes it, and even collaborates on other people's projects as a producer on the side. He says that you don't need an expensive studio; he does everything in his room with Logic Pro X.

Landon's take on the royalties and streaming services is a bit more optimistic than Thom's, but they both have the same fundamental advice. Only make music if that's what you love.

Me: *On what platforms do you offer your music? How do they compare?*

Landon: *I'm on all streaming platforms. I have tons of songs; I dropped 21 just last year [2018]. Spotify seems to be what's really breaking artists these days with the playlists and all. A lot of people use Apple Music, but I'd say Spotify is winning because of the playlist trends and the affiliation with the major labels feeding them. People seem to be complaining about the streams and the money you make, but you make more than you think—those clicks add up. Plus, people don't really buy music anymore, so it's like, take it or leave it.*

Me: *Do you have to keep creating new music in order to keep making money?*

Landon: *This generation is extremely content-driven. In this era, you MUST have content. Music consumers, as a whole, need to take more time to appreciate things instead of living in this 24/7 media-driven spiral. An artist has to make content to stay relevant. I'm a content guy. I don't like sitting around too long without dropping something; it's just not me.*

Me: *How passive would you say music is as an income source?*

Landon: *The good thing is that once the songs are out, it's passive income, and you can let them ride. The more songs, the better. It's a ton of work to get it out, depending on your expectations of the art. But it totally depends. I'm very selfish with my art, so I want it to be exactly like I want it. It takes a long time sometimes, but I've had times where I make a song and drop it literally that night. Usually, it's a lot of work though. I won't lie. You gotta think about getting the distribution uploaded, the artwork, release date, all that.*

Me: *Would you recommend that others try to pursue this avenue as a passive income stream?*

Landon: *If your heart's in it, absolutely. Just create something genuine, and don't try to make something for a quick money grab because it won't happen. You gotta really build it up to get paid in this industry.*

Thank you, Landon! Make sure to follow Landon Sears on social media at:

Instagram: www.instagram.com/searslikethestore

Twitter: www.twitter.com/landonator

*out, it's passive income, and you can let them ride.*

## In Summary:

Let me give it to you straight: Royalties earned from music can be a very challenging passive income stream to pursue. Just like with writing a book, success takes talent, hard work, passion, and often luck. If you're not already a musician who's willing to do whatever it takes, it might be wise to swipe left on this particular royalty income. If you *are* venturing down this route anyway, then I hope you have found this information valuable. You need to really love creating music to monetize it.

In the next chapter, we're going to talk about three fun and unique types of royalties: photography, downloadable content, and Print-on-Demand.

# CHAPTER 9

# Photos, Downloads, and PODs

**P**hotography

Nope, I'm not talking wedding photographer, baby photographer, or senior portrait photographer. Those definitely aren't passive. They take a specific person's talent, and that person has to be somewhere for a certain amount of time to generate income. That type of photography is most certainly active income.

To generate passive royalties from photography, you upload and license your photos on a stock image website. First, what is stock photography? Stock images are inexpensive, high-quality photos that people buy to use for advertising, business, websites, blogs, and projects. Stock photos generally depict common landscapes, people, nature, and events. Think of generic images you see on brochures, posters, and websites. Likely, those are all stock photos.

Some popular websites where you can buy and sell your stock photos are iStock, Getty Images, Shutterstock, BigStockPhoto, and 500pxPrime.

You can purchase photographs as a buyer or license them as a seller in many different ways, and each comes with different rights. As a buyer, you must read the fine print in the user agreement to know exactly what you can do with the photo. Are you only allowed to use it once (in ONE social media post, or on ONE website), or can you use it over and over again? If you buy it, does that make you the exclusive user of the photo? Or can other people also buy and use it?

As a seller of photography, these terms will be equally important. After all, if you are selling photographs on a site that only offers exclusive rights to buyers (meaning each photo can be sold or licensed to only ONE buyer), you will have to continue uploading photos all the time so that you don't run out of inventory.

On the other hand, if you are selling on a site that only offers non-exclusive images, then other users may also pay to license the same image. One photograph can be licensed over and over again and potentially earn income forever. *That's* what you're going for with this passive income stream.

BigStockPhoto operates in the latter way. You can upload hundreds of images, and if they do well and continue to sell, you can sit back and collect royalties.

Don't underestimate how difficult this will be. It sounds easy to throw a bunch of photos online and sit back and wait for money. If that's how it really works, why isn't everyone doing it?

An important component of success is talent, experience, know-how... whatever you want to call it. Photography is an intense market these days. I can go online and look for an image for my next book cover and, quite literally, find hundreds of thousands of options. How will you set yourself apart? At a bare minimum, you need to have a high-quality camera, know how to use it, have professional editing software, be *good* at editing, and find a way to create something new and unique. What do you offer that's different from every other photographer?

If you are talented, hard-working, willing to learn marketing, and can offer something new or different to the marketplace to set yourself apart, royalties from stock photography could be a great option for you!

## Downloadable content

Like other passive income streams, downloadable content is something you create once and sell over and over again. It's typically stored online and downloaded by potential users or customers.

Here are several examples:

- Prints (photography, drawings, any other type of art)
- Invitations (wedding, baby shower, bridal shower, birthday party, any sort of event)
- Worksheets (income and expense tracker, contracts)
- Templates (To-Do lists, weekly planners, calendars, resume templates, certificates, awards, embroidery templates)
- Event tickets, menus, gift tags

All who have planned a wedding say, "Aye Do." First, hats off to you. I got engaged in 2017, tried to start planning a wedding twelve months later, and promptly gave up. Too much money and stress for me! (I did still get married, sorry fellas.)

One thing I remember doing is scoping out the cost of ordering wedding invitations. I asked people online what they paid, and most said a few hundred dollars, with many paying over $500. It gets expensive when you order fancy-schmancy prints from Minted or Shutterstock. Alternatively, some people I know saved costs by downloading a template from Etsy or another online store, filling it in on their computer with all the details, and then printing it themselves at FedEx, Costco, or even on their very own printer on stock paper. Brilliant! They paid a one-time fee for the template they wanted and handled the printing costs on their own, and in the end, it was way cheaper.

Think about the person who sold them this template. This person has the artistic skills to create a beautiful wedding invitation and list it on Etsy or another website. Let's say it's priced at $20. Instead of selling a physical item on Etsy one time for $20, they are selling a digital item over and over again for $20. That same downloadable template can be sold ten, twenty, fifty times over, and they don't even have to lift a finger. Fifty sales at $20 each is $1,000. And that's just from *one* template. What if they have eighty templates, each selling fifty per year for $20 a pop? Drum roll, please...

that's $80,000! Wow, that was much more than I thought it was going to be. Obviously, you have to subtract Etsy's fees and all that, but still. You can see how downloadable content is a very attractive passive income idea.

Wedding invitation templates are possibly overdone by now. Think about one of our Factors of SCRIMP: marketability. Is there a demand for a wedding invitation? Definitely. But is the market already saturated? Is there already an enormous supply? What's the competition like? I personally wouldn't pursue this route because it feels very "been there, done that," and I don't want to compete with 9,000 other people on Etsy doing the same thing. (Chapter 6 on market research is essential, people!)

Ideas for downloadable content are unlimited. Revert to the list above for inspiration or start making your own list of potential moneymakers. Take any one of those ideas and make it specific. What about gift tags specifically for gifts given to women getting a divorce? What about food-themed embroidery templates? What about certificates that parents can print out for their kids when they do certain chores or complete certain tasks? The more specific your target audience, the better. You'll have less competition and really get to zero in on your audience's needs.

Etsy is not the only marketplace for this. Check out the website for Creative Market, which sells "ready-to-use design assets from independent creators." It's the same idea, but a little more specific. You could find all sorts of online avenues in which you can sell this downloadable content. Once you get some sales under your belt, you can even create your own website and drive traffic there too.

Like other royalties, you'll put a lot of time into Stage 1 to create and launch your downloadable content. Then in Stage 2, after you build momentum, you'll spend less time maintaining the income.

## Print-on-Demand

### How it works

Print-on-Demand is a fun passive income idea and one that I have personal experience with. Imagine the last hoodie or baseball cap you bought. Did it have a sports team, logo, or some other branded image? Take, for example, a hat with the Detroit Lions logo. Guess what? Detroit Lions, Inc. owns both that phrase *and* logo. Whoever sold you that hat has to pay them a share of the profits (a *royalty.*) So, every year, Detroit Lions, Inc. gets paid money from manufacturers, chain stores, boutique stores, websites, and anyone else that uses their logo. Detroit Lions, Inc. isn't necessarily physically involved with making the products and selling them, but they still make money. They get paid simply from owning a trademark. How's that for passive income?

*Print-on-demand eliminates inventory risk. You get paid only if and when the product sells. It's brilliant!*

I'm not saying you should go figure out how to buy that trademark from them, but you can earn money in a similar way by creating designs to sell on articles of clothing, mugs, pens, you name it.

Allow me to introduce you to Print-On-Demand (POD). A POD platform does exactly what it sounds like: it prints items on the spot. When you think about how all those Detroit Lions shirts or hats or jerseys get made, you first start with the article of clothing, and then you somehow adhere the logo or image or phrase onto it. One can apply an image to an object with Direct to Garment (DTG), screen printing, embroidery, and so forth.

POD is an enormous advantage to you from a risk perspective. Think about opening a store and selling physical items. To ensure success, you'd have to put a lot of time into upfront research so that you can be *sure* that your items will sell. Because if they don't, you're screwed. After all, you're putting money into designing these items, into production, and, most of all, into inventory. As a creator of physical items, carrying an inventory always involves some level of risk. If your inventory doesn't sell, you take a loss. Period.

POD, on the other hand, takes the inventory out of the game altogether. When a customer sees your product and wants to order it, you print one for them on-demand, once the order is placed. You *print as you go*. No more carrying inventories of 3,000 phone cases that might never sell. Instead, you produce your products *after* you get the order or sale. It's brilliant, right?

Not only does POD eliminate inventory risk, but it also eliminates marketing risk. You no longer need to know what will or won't sell up front. You simply think of ideas, offer them to the world, and get paid only on what sells. POD is beautiful.

So, let's combine these two ideas. First, we have the idea of earning money off of designs that go on products, not the products themselves. Then, we have the idea of POD. Together, they are a home run.

## POD Platforms

Everyday people are doing POD by using online platforms. You sign up, set up your account, create and upload designs *onto products that the platform itself offers for sale*, and then get paid only when products sell.

If this excites you, take a moment and check out the following websites:

- Threadless
- Teespring
- Redbubble
- Merch
- Zazzle
- TeeFury
- Printful & Etsy
- Fine Art America
- Society6
- SunFrog
- Shopify and Amazon with Teelaunch
- CafePress

Each of these websites offers a slightly different platform for getting into the POD business. Each has its own pros and cons. Some charge you a signup fee just to use their platform. Some charge a recurring monthly fee. I try to stay away from those because I don't want to risk having a bunch of designs uploaded that aren't selling well and then being forced to pay a fee regardless.

Some have large audiences, some small. Some offer hundreds of different types of products, while others offer only a few. Each platform offers a different royalty split. You'll want to compare exactly how much you'll make off of each sale because it can vary greatly. It's normally not a lot; maybe a few dollars, maybe more, maybe less. I have personally used Redbubble, Printful & Etsy, and Merch, and I am looking into others.

## Designs

Ladies and gents, this is a numbers game. If you throw eight designs up and decide you're done, I doubt you'll get far (unless one of them goes viral.) The more designs you have, the more likely someone is to find something they like.

Let's say that, for every twenty designs you create, you get one sale. Let's say that once you get that first sale, the design continues to sell about once per month. Let's say you earn a $3 royalty on average. That means that twenty designs uploaded equate to $3 per month. Now, multiply by a hundred. Two thousand designs uploaded equates to $300 per month. That's more like it.

Yes, two thousand designs is a lot. I'm not saying it will absolutely take two thousand designs to make $300 per month. Your earnings will vary greatly depending on your platform, design quality, product offering, and royalty split. But you get the point; the more designs you upload, the more money you will make because you will have that many more chances of something selling. As of today (2019), my highest-profit month from my POD business netted me about $1,700.

Make sure that every design is going on as many different products as possible. If you're going to take the time to upload it onto a tote bag, then you should upload it onto other products your platform offers too. After all, someone might not like your flamingo tote bag, but maybe they'll love your flamingo laptop case.

Designs come in all shapes and sizes. Inspiration is all over the place. Just by scrolling through Facebook, you might see a funny meme, phrase, or quote. Write it down. Start a list of design ideas. Go shopping. Look at shirts at Walmart. Look at mugs at Kroger. Look at everything in Target. Use these as sources of inspiration. Surf the web. Look on websites that sell products. Look around you. What are your friends wearing? What products do you own that have designs on them? Take a trip to your closet, your kitchen, your walls.

Some designs are text-based, and some are graphic. Make sure to create a list of design ideas with columns for each category. You can see which type sells better and focus solely on creating those.

Be careful not to infringe on copyright or trademark laws. You can't put "Nike" on a design. Beware of Disney. You can't put the name of anything at all that is trademarked. That includes board games, brands, sports teams, etc. Generally, avoiding pronouns altogether is a good call.

Even harmless phrases might be trademarked for use on products. You really never know, so just make sure that you double-check everything you create on the United States Patent & Trademark Office (USPTO) website.

## DIY vs. Hiring a Freelancer

So, the big question is obviously: how do I actually make designs? Photoshop and Lightroom, baby.

If you're artistic, I highly recommend creating content yourself. Go one-by-one down your design list and start creating. It will take a lot of time at first, but once you get the hang of it, you can start whipping out designs within a few minutes—especially if they are text-based.

Chances are, the platform you use will have specifications for your designs. They might require a specific pixel size, file size, or even colors. Make sure you start by setting up a template for yourself that you can use over and over again, that way you don't have to worry about the specs each time.

Think of what your design will look like if viewed at thumbnail size and focus on creating clear, bright, bold colors and lines that will stand out. Make sure the image itself is positioned well within your template. Even if you're not super Photoshop savvy, text-based designs can easily be created by yourself with enough practice.

On the other hand, maybe you either don't know how to create designs or don't want to. Great! Hire somebody on Fiverr or Upwork to do it for you.

When you're looking for a designer, start by creating a job specification. What exactly do you want? How long do you want to give them to get it done? What are the specifications for the designs? You should write out everything that they'll need to know. Then, you can shop around using your job spec document and asking for quotes from different freelancers.

You'll want to view the freelancer's past work. Make sure that they aren't stealing other artists' work or using clipart from the Internet (Google reverse image search does wonders for this). You want to find an artist whose designs are original, attractive, and high-quality.

Consider price. You might just be starting, but you need to put together at least some type of estimate for what you think your royalty would be and how many designs you think it will take to sell something. We'll be more optimistic this time and, as an example, we'll say that one out of every ten designs sells, and once it sells once, it continues to sell once per week, and your royalty is $5. This means that for every ten designs you upload, you'll earn $20 per month.

If the person you find on Fiverr or Upwork wants to charge $25 per design, does that make sense for you financially? You'll be paying them $250 for ten designs, knowing that ten designs will net you $20 per month. That means it will take you over a year to break even. Thank you, next.

It's not a good use of money to start hiring and uploading designs without running the numbers. There's no right or wrong answer on a breakeven point, but you need to figure out what YOU are willing to do. If your breakeven point is two months, then in the scenario above, you would only be willing to pay $4 per design. Careful; that might be too *low*. Maybe no designer you talk to would be willing to do that. I'm just playing devil's advocate here. Test the waters and go by your budget.

I'll step off my soapbox so that we can move on to the next royalty idea: online courses.

# CHAPTER 10

# Dropping Your Knowledge with Online Courses

Online courses exist in all shapes and sizes. You can take an online college course, follow a bodybuilding program, or sign up for an Intro to Excel course. The possibilities are endless.

Stages 1 and 2 of royalty-generating online courses are exactly the same as launching a book. You invest time up front to create and launch the course, and then it's out there forever for people to find and buy. That's when you can step back and rake in the royalties.

I'm considering pursuing this passive income stream myself by creating an online real estate investing course. More on real estate investing later, but I believe it could be valuable to my readers to offer an in-depth, hands-on guide for how to get started with rental property investing, including leases and screening documents and everything else a newbie would need.

Online courses can be taught using many different mediums: audio lectures, video lectures, pictures, templates for downloading, quizzes, and more. And since they are so much more involved and offer more than a book ever could, the end-user generally would pay more money for a course than they would a book.

While you can create your own website and sell the course yourself, you can also sign up for a website specifically designed for course creators. They will make things extremely easy, and they sometimes already have an enormous page viewership, which means it will be easier for you to get your course in front of people who want to buy it. Each course platform is slightly different and offers differing royalty options. A few of the most popular platforms for creating and selling courses are:

- Udemy
- Teachable
- Skillshare
- Thinkific
- Kajabi
- Podia

Here are a few things to consider in determining which platform to use to create your course:

1) Where will your students come from? Most of these platforms simply offer course-building features. As it stands now, Udemy and Skillshare are the only marketplaces, meaning they have a large student base. All of the other platforms would require you to direct your own students to sign up for your courses. You'll have to market yourself either way, but it could be a little easier to sell your course in a marketplace-style platform. Also, if you don't bring your own students, will you be able to follow up with them via email? That is, do you "own" your students?

2) How does the pricing work? Does the platform charge you a flat fee or a percentage of revenue? Does the pricing change with the number of students and courses you offer? Will you be charged transaction fees? Think about what will be vital to your course's success in the long-term.

3) What features does the platform offer? Are you able to integrate with any other websites or email marketing platforms (like

Mailchimp, for example)? Will you be able to accept international students? Can you create a landing page? Can you set up affiliates to help sell your course? Can you test students with quizzes? There's a slew of features out there, and they vary widely between each platform.

## How To

Creating an online course takes much of the same effort and strategy as writing a book.

The content itself will be slightly different than that of a book. A book is made up of written chapters. A course is made up of sections or modules and could involve text, video, audio, quizzes, or any other type of content. Courses are inherently more interactive and engaging.

First, use the tactics in Chapter 6 to come up with a killer course idea. Once you narrow down your content and you know what you want your course to be about, you can start creating it. Most of the platforms I've listed above have a free version or some sort of free trial where you can test out their platform. Keep the following tips in mind:

1) Don't make the course too long: People's attention spans are incredibly short, especially in our high-tech, social media-driven world. Shorter is better, as in 15 to 30 minutes. Many courses are even broken up into clips that are five minutes each. Long-form courses should be ninety minutes tops, and if you're going to make it long, split it into chunks or modules so that students can easily take a break or find a stopping point.

2) Price the course correctly: Information content courses can range from $10 to $1,000+, so it can be difficult to know how to price your course. At the bare minimum, I recommend pricing your course at $100. If you feel like that's high, remember, having fewer but more engaged students is better than having hundreds of less-committed students paying $15 each. Higher pricing means higher quality students. If you feel that's too low, by all means, increase your pricing. It's not uncommon for a real estate investing course to run in the four figures. And it really helps to offer a payment plan so that students don't have to pay the whole thing at once. Podia

did a study that showed the average price of a course in their dataset was $182.59.[34] Both Podia and Teachable have tons of articles, calculators, and resources that can help you price your course correctly.

Much like you would with a book, it's best to outline the entire course beforehand. Start with the specific course aim. How would you sum up the benefits of taking your course in one sentence? From there, you can outline the main modules. Make sure your course is specific. For example, I wouldn't be able to create a course about passive income. As you can see, it's taken me an entire book to introduce the subject, and I could've included another 200 pages! But I could create a course about finding your first rental property because it's more focused.

Outline the content first, then identify how you'll deliver the content. Will this section be a video lesson? Will this module be a screen share? Would a quiz be valuable here? Once you have the content and delivery outlined, you can create it.

## A Case Study: Bobby Hoyt, Entrepreneur and Founder of *Millennial Money Man*

Ladies and gents, I'm delighted to introduce you to Bobby Hoyt, founder of *Millennial Money Man*. Bobby is one of the most bada$$ people I know. A few years ago, he was a high school band director in Houston, TX, and became frustrated working seventy to eighty hours per week knowing his annual income increase wasn't even beating inflation. He also had $40,000 of student loans he was trying to pay off, which inspired him to start his M$M blog.

Today, Bobby is making six figures *per month* from all types of passive income streams: ads, affiliate marketing, online courses, and recurring membership revenue. For this case study, we'll zero in on his online course revenue, which generates $50,000 to $100,000 *per month* in passive income.

Where did Bobby get the idea for his first course? In his own words: *I started talking to an old friend from high school named Mike Yanda, who runs a Facebook ad agency full-time. He mentioned that I should teach my audience how to run FB ads for local businesses in their spare time,* because it pays well, doesn't take a ton of time, and can be scaled to a full agency over time. I was running Facebook ads for my marketing clients, so I realized that it was probably a good idea to share that with my audience. Mike and I created the course together and launched it to my audience in Jan. 2018. We did $130,000 (!) in one weekend realized that we were on something big.

Bobby currently offers courses: the one mentioned at where he teaches people hov make an extra $1,000 to $2, per month running Facebook for local businesses, and another course that teaches bloggers how

> *[We] created the course together and launched it to my audience in Jan. 2018. We did $130,000 (!) in one weekend...*

to run paid traffic campaigns to grow their audiences. (If either of those pique your interest, you can learn more in your *PIAR* Bonus Gift at **www.moneyhoneyrachel.com/bonus**.)

So, the golden question: how passive is it? Bobby explains:

*In the beginning, I'd say that this was not passive at all. It was HARD work. But as time has gone on, it has become much more passive. These days, we have our sales process automated through email campaigns and Facebook ad systems. Those run in the background and would likely continue to generate revenue if we didn't lift a finger for the next year. But Mike and I enjoy running the business, and we regularly create content and put work in to continue to grow it.*

In other words: Bobby is working to continue growing his income; otherwise, he could step away completely, and sales would keep coming in at the current level.

When I asked Bobby what people should know about passive income, this is what he said:

*It's rarely passive in the beginning (and sometimes never truly passive but can get pretty close). You have to create the assets and systems to keep revenue coming in without you, which takes a lot of time initially. But once you lay the foundation, you can truly make money while you sleep. I've had plenty of days where I've made thousands of dollars per*

*In the beginning... this was not passive at all... But once you lay the foundation, you can truly make money while you sleep. I've had plenty of days where I've made thousands of dollars per day on vacation.* **„**

-Bobby Hoyt

day on vacation. Then, if you're wired to work like I am, you just keep stacking income streams on top of each other and diversify to whatever seems fun/challenging to you.

You can check out Bobby's website at www.millennialmoneyman.com and make sure to follow him on social media.

Facebook: www.facebook.com/genymoneyman

Instagram: www.instagram.com/genymoneyman

Twitter: www.twitter.com/GenYMoneyMan

# CHAPTER 11

# Software, Franchising, Minerals, Oh My!

These next three royalty income ideas can be elusive. They require special skills and/or materials that are not accessible to most people. However, these business-oriented royalty incomes can certainly be passive and profitable, so here we go!

## Software & Apps

I know nothing (Jon Snow) about coding, computers, or IT, so I'll leave the technical talk to the pros. The basics of this passive income stream involve developing software and licensing it for sale or creating an app and offering it as a paid download. Anytime someone buys or uses your product, you receive a royalty.

Think about the Microsoft Office suite, which, according to BusinessDictionary.com, is the most common form of software used in the western world. Anyone that wants to buy the software can purchase it and install it on his or her computer. Anytime someone purchases it, Paul Allen and Bill Gates, the founders, are paid a royalty.

What about the App Store? The App Store has free apps, paid apps, and subscription-based apps. Free apps generally earn money through ad revenue, while paid apps earn money anytime someone purchases or downloads them. Subscription-based apps are the jackpot, as they earn money recurrently.

You can create all different kinds of software or apps: news, games, information, marketplaces (think Tinder), ride-sharing, delivery services... apps that integrate with the real-world, apps that are for entertainment on your smartphone only... your only limit is your imagination. Just the other day, my mom came up with the idea of an app that can have a drone deliver you a gas can in case you ever run out of gas and are stranded. She may be getting a bit too ambitious with this futuristic idea, but it's an interesting one!

If you are an uber-smart tech person and you have the skills to create something that would be valuable to people, this would be an insanely awesome route to take. Not many people have that kind of knowledge, so if you can pair that with the ability to fill a market need, you're golden.

If you don't know anything about coding, but you think your idea is good enough, don't let your lack of knowledge stop you. You can enroll in free or paid courses to learn about coding, you can download Apple's free Xcode (a complete toolset for developing apps), or you can hire a contractor or freelancer to do it for you.

With app development, you will need to invest time to create, market, and launch it, and then once you see some success and get it going, you won't have to be as actively involved. That's when it becomes passive income.

## Franchising

Do you ever wonder what it takes to open a Chick-Fil-A? I think about it a lot, actually, probably because I often find myself in the Chick-Fil-A drive through doing the math of how many orders per minute they must get during lunch and what the average order is, in an attempt to estimate their total revenue. My brain is weird.

When someone opens a Chick-Fil-A, they are opening a franchise. A franchise is a license granted by a business owner to open a branch of a business. The Cathy family, who owns all that delicious chicken goodness, opened the first Chick-Fil-A in 1967. From there, they might have opened a few more. At some point, they realized they couldn't keep opening and operating Chick-Fil-As themselves, so they offered an option for another person to franchise their business. That person would be able to open a Chick-Fil-A in return for payment to the Cathy family. Once the Cathys began offering the opportunity to franchise, Chick-Fil-As began opening left and right. Because of franchising, Chick-Fil-A opened its 2000th store in 2016.

To open a franchise of a business, you normally have to pay a large upfront fee in addition to a portion of your revenue or profits to the business owner.

What I am proposing is not to *open* a franchise. It's to *offer* a franchise.

If you have a business idea that's scalable, repeatable, and not geographically confined, franchising might be perfect for you.

The business itself must be relatively passive, at least for you. Restaurants—Chick-Fil-A included—are very active, often requiring the owner or general manager to put in seventy-hour-weeks.

What if you start tutoring high school kids in Spanish? Maybe your friend wants to do something similar, and you match him up with another high school kid. You teach your friend how tutor and give him some materials a resources. Your friend gets going and pays yo percentage of his revenue since you provided materials, helped him find a student to tut and continued to support him. That's essential premise of a franchise. You keep do this until you realize you're running a tutor business. You have five tutors who each tuto of every single tutoring session since the tutors rely on you for your materials, expertise, and business acumen. Cool!

> **Don't open a franchise.**
>
> **Offer a franchise.**

Think about how to legitimately franchise a service you offer or a business you're thinking about starting. Can you come up with a business plan and teach it to someone else? Is there another market nearby that needs something similar? Do you get people coming up to you and asking you how you started your business all the time? Offer to franchise it. They pay you an upfront fee (typically, it's thousands of dollars, but it depends on the business) AND ongoing royalties in return for your business plan, know-how, and coaching. Get a few of those up and running, and then you can start to step back and reap the rewards. There are lots of franchises you may not have thought about, including (but not limited to) car detailing, housekeeping, moving, tailoring, etc.

Franchising isn't a likely option for most, but I wanted to include it in the chance it could apply to you. Simply re-evaluating things as a producer instead of a consumer, thinking about yourself as a franchiser instead of a franchisee, and operating from an owner-perspective will open up many, many doors for you.

Time investment? High. Money investment? Not necessarily anything. Passivity? Completely depends. Depending on the type of business, I believe you can get creative and find a way to offer a franchise by only spending a couple of hours per week. It won't work for every single scenario, but it can be hugely lucrative.

## Mineral Rights: A Briefing

One of the more obscure types of royalty I want to mention is mineral rights. In most of the world, when someone owns property, they only own the surface of the property, meaning the top layer of the land. But in the US, individuals can actually own mineral rights as well, which are rights to any natural resources *under* the surface. Yep, we can own our grass *and* our dirt.

Grass doesn't generate income, but oil does. Coal does. Granite does. Minerals do.

There's a lotttt of money in rock and dirt, people!

Owners of mineral rights can lease those rights to a corporation or entity that wants access to those valuable natural resources. Normally, the mineral rights owner will get a lease bonus payment upfront, or a royalty of everything that's extracted, or both. As long as the agreement is in place, the owner will be paid royalties.

To first find out whether you own the mineral rights under your land, you can get a copy of your deed, or you can go to your county clerk's office where the land is located, or you can hire a title company to do a title search on the mineral rights ownership. You should also research what kinds of natural resources exist where you live. What might be common in Texas might not be common in Maine.

If you own your mineral rights and are in an abundant area, this could be a literal goldmine for you.

CHAPTER 12

# The Must-Know on Marketing & Launching

Royalty-generating income streams for the win! By now, you've learned all about how to create the nine main types of royalties:

1) Books and eBooks

2) Music

3) Photography

4) Downloadable Content

5) Print-On-Demand

6) Online courses

7) Software or app development

8) Franchising

9) Mineral Rights

Once you've educated yourself, brainstormed, created the product, and put in the work, how do you *sell it?*

In this chapter, we'll discuss the importance of marketing, outline some specific marketing strategies, and talk about how to get reviews and testimonials.

## The Importance of Marketing

The ONE thing that music, books, photography, downloadable content, products, online courses, software, and apps all have in common is that their success depends on sales. And sales, my dear friend, depends on marketing.

The reality is, you could write the world's catchiest song that falls flat because you don't do any marketing; alternatively, you could write a decent song that becomes a hit because you kicked a$$ at promoting it. People won't listen to it if they don't know it exists!

You can't expect to upload a bunch of stock photos and suddenly make $2,000 a month. Nope. You have to promote your photos and get your work out there. That's what marketing is for: getting your stuff out there. Showing people what you have to offer. Enticing people to buy. Generating leads and sales. Sure, you might get some organic sales and interest from whatever website or platform you're using, but if you really want to be successful, you won't undermine the importance of self-promotion. After all, you don't want to spend hours taking, editing, and uploading photos never to make a sale!

*Sales is not a meritocracy. It's not the **best** thing that necessarily sells the most; it is the thing hat is best marketed.*

To be clear: the success of your product depends on your marketing, so you'll want to take this part *very* seriously. Sales is not a meritocracy. It's not the *best* thing that necessarily sells the most; it is the thing that is best marketed.

Learning how to market is simply another step in the process of creating royalty streams. Don't underestimate it, but don't let it intimidate you. Marketing is essential. If your creation flops, it's probably because you didn't have a good enough marketing plan in place.

The reason I've had such success with my books and my designs is that I market them well. If I didn't, I wouldn't be writing this book. I did not major in marketing. My skills are self-taught with a side of intuition. You can learn a ton about marketing by reading free articles and blogs online. Or you can invest in a social media marketing course, buy a lead generation book, or pay someone to do it for you. Don't let a lack of marketing knowledge stop you. Not a lot of people know how to do it unless they learned it somewhere.

## Basic Marketing Strategies

Update your audience. When I launched *Money Honey*, I started by announcing to friends and family that I was writing a book. While that may just feel like an update, it's actually a type of marketing. I was getting word of my product out there. Tell people what you are doing! Update them on your process, your updates, your fears, and your challenges. You can do this in person with your friend groups, church, book club, work, or gym class. The best place to engage your audience is on social media.

Start a social media following. In the weeks and months leading up to your product launch, start a Facebook Page, Instagram, and Twitter account. Invite all of your family and friends to like your page and follow you. Then, you can post updates on your POD product, your new software, or your new stock photography biz. You can give sneak peeks, post funny memes, or make fun, informative posts that are related to your topic. Post consistently throughout Stage 1. Feel free to follow my *Money Honey Rachel* Facebook page or Instagram to see some of the ways I market myself and my books.

Join Facebook groups for research. If you can reach your target audience on Facebook, then find a group related to your royalty-generating idea and post for the sake of doing research. For example, if you're designing embroidery templates that people can download on Etsy, join Facebook groups that discuss embroidery. Once you post and comment in the group often enough, people will be invested in your product and excited to help you succeed. I asked a lot of questions and got great feedback in some Facebook groups when writing *Money Honey*. It was actually unintentional from a marketing perspective, but little did I know that engaging in Facebook groups was a form of marketing too and that it was creating interest in my book. You can even involve people on social media in picking out the title of your business, your logo, and any other big decisions by doing surveys and asking for feedback. The more involved your friends are, the more they will want to help you succeed.

Consider advertising to reach your target audience. *If* you want to spend money on advertising, you'll want to figure out how and where to do that. If you're about to release a new single, can you promote it on Spotify or create an Instagram ad? If you're launching a POD product, can you create sponsored ads on Facebook? I decided against spending money to promote my first book, *Money Honey*. To this day, I have not spent a cent on advertising; *Money Honey* sells by word-of-mouth. But I created an ad budget for *PIAR* since I'm more confident in my abilities and have a small following. There are all sorts of websites and newsletters that exist solely to promote eBooks, so that's where a lot of my dollars are going for this launch. You can hire a copywriter or marketing pro if you need help creating powerful ad copy.

Market your product locally. Consider other marketing efforts you can perform in your area. Is your online course related to health and nutrition? If so, can you find healthy markets, juicing stores, and protein shake stores and collaborate with them? Is your audiobook about best practices and safety procedures for car- or ride-sharing? If so, can you go to the airport or to the bars at night and hand out business cards or pamphlets?

Get creative. You can Google other marketing ideas and create an entire list for yourself and focus on doing two new things per week during Stage 1 as you create your product. It's important to start marketing efforts early on, well before launch. That way, by the time you launch, you will already have a solid marketing platform, and tons of people will be waiting to buy your product.

## Pre-launch and Beta Testing

The pre-launch and beta testing strategies are something I specifically learned when I was researching online courses, but we can also apply them to many of the other types of royalty income.

When launching content, it helps to have a following or platform. Any trust or credibility you can build with your audience beforehand will help. If you don't have that, you can still launch a successful product.

A pre-launch builds buzz and generates interest before you make the product officially available. The first step in your pre-launch is building your email list. Social media is especially effective in generating interest. You can announce your intentions, tell people about your course, and direct them to an email signup form. MailChimp works wonders to collect emails of interested people, and you can also create a landing page using Wix or Squarespace to keep people updated on your product.

Then you can continue to promote your product through teaser content. This should be primarily visual content, like videos or pictures, that gives people an idea of what to expect and how they'll benefit by using your product.

Beta testing is another pre-launch strategy where you offer part of your content for free or at a discounted rate to get both feedback and testimonials. This strategy can be used for books, eBooks, audiobooks, online courses, or any other content-driven royalty. A beta launch can give you valuable information about what works and what doesn't so that you can go back and make tweaks and additions before the official launch.

## Launch Group

In terms of the success of my first book *Money Honey,* I'd credit 30% to great content and 70% to a great launch. If I didn't have a clear, ambitious, well-laid-out launch plan, my book wouldn't have done nearly as well. Please don't make the mistake of thinking that just because you have a great product, people will buy it. No, no, NO. You have to figure out how to make people WANT to buy it. #RantOver.

If you have the option with your product and platform, I highly recommend a free launch. For a short period of time, when you first release the product, you offer it for free. For content creators with a small or no following, this is absolutely the best route. It's hard to get people to pay for something if you don't have any credibility. Plus, it's all about momentum and reach. Yes, maybe you are giving up some initial royalty income, but you are gaining a lot more: a massive number of followers. And these are people that will come back to buy more from you if you let them!

For example, if you are self-publishing a book on Amazon, you have the option of offering your eBook for free for up to five days. I chose to launch *Money Honey* for free for about a three-day period and offered the paperback at a pretty low price of $9.95. From there, I increased the price by about $1.00 per week until I found the sweet spot where I was making the most money, and readers felt the information I provided was worth the investment.

No matter the type of product, before you launch, you'll want to assemble your launch group. This group of people is invested in your success and wants to help you launch your product. Your family and friends are pretty much a given, but you'll want to recruit as many people as possible. You can offer your launch group perks like early access to your product or exclusive insider content.

Being in your launch group means committing to helping you succeed. You can ask your launch group to try out and use your product (at a discount!), leave a review, and share the word on social media.

## Getting Reviews

Your product's launch depends on both sales and reviews. On the day of (and even before) your launch, you should try to get as many online reviews and testimonials as possible. One way to do this is by giving your launch group access to your product for free ahead of time. With books, writers can send out Advanced Reader Copies. These advanced readers will then have access to leave a review early. I did this with *Money Honey* and had 15 reviews prior to launch! When strangers or random people saw my book, they already thought it was credible.

On the day of launch, encourage your launch group and post on social media asking people to leave you a review. Further, text your family and friends to let them know that it's launch day and that you would appreciate them checking out your product and leaving a review. I also privately messaged Facebook friends and acquaintances. I was not afraid to ask for the review. Because of the initial influx of reviews, my book did very well.

Make sure that you ask your consumers to leave you a review, too. Insert a letter at the end of your course or book or set up an email opt-in so you can follow up with anyone that buys your product. You can also set up an automated email campaign so that after one week, they are reminded to leave you a review.

## Post-Launch

The overall goal with your product is to have an enormous, successful launch that will enable sales to propel forward. The launch should set off your momentum so that you continue to attract and retain new customers as you go. As you can see, this passive income stream requires a very large upfront time investment, and once it's launched, it's a matter of having some marketing in place so that you continue to attract customers. You can do this yourself, or you can hire a social media marketer to make the passive income stream truly passive.

## Conclusion

I love royalty income streams. It's one of the coolest passive income ideas out there. They don't *require* an upfront investment of money. That's great because it means *anyone* can do this. Royalty streams do require an upfront investment of time, not only in building and creating the offering but in marketing and launching it. Then you get to sit back and relax in Stage 2, where you put in minimal effort and time to maintain the income stream with marketing activities. Success with royalties takes a committed, determined, marketing-savvy person. And I genuinely believe that anyone can do it.

Royalty income can be so wonderfully fulfilling! That's why I love it. You are creating a product or service that someone needs—that helps someone. There's nothing more exciting than filling a market need and helping people.

Next, we'll look at a totally different type of passive income. The next passive income type requires a substantial upfront investment of money but requires absolutely no time or additional work. It is the most passive income stream we'll discuss!

> *I love royalty income streams... They don't require an upfront investment of money. That's great because it means anyone can do this.*

# SECTION THREE:
# Portfolio Income

## CHAPTER 13

# *Portfolio Income: The Basics*

**The What**

Moving right along to one of the most passive income streams, AKA portfolio income. As we said earlier, portfolio income is from dividends, interest, investments, and capital gains. The basic premise of creating this passive income stream is to have an enormous chunk of money that you can invest, and then live off the interest or dividend income. Portfolio income requires quite the opposite of the time-intensive royalty income stream: it requires money.

Portfolio income is such a great passive income stream because it requires no work in Stage 2. But to generate portfolio income in the first place, you need a ton of capital. In Stage 1, you just need to invest your capital properly, and it will start generating income right away. Portfolio income is what people mean when they say, "Put your money to work!" or "Make your money work for you!"

A quick recap on some stock market terminology. By the way, I go over the basics of investing in much more detail in my book, *Money Honey*. If you are a total beginner, I highly encourage you to start there.

*...rtfolio income is what people mean when they say, 'Put your money to work!' or 'Make your money work for you!'*

Stock: A piece of ownership in a company. Buying a company's stock makes you a shareholder.

Exchange-Traded Fund (ETF): A collection of different stocks in a single fund. ETFs trade just like stocks and cost much less than mutual funds.

Bond: A bond represents a debt. A company or entity borrows money from you in the form of a bond and pays you interest. You are the lender.

Certificate of Deposit (CD): A type of savings account where you agree to keep a set amount of money deposited at your bank for a set amount of time, in return for interest.

Dividend: Money that a company pays out of its profits to its shareholders. It's paid in regular, typically quarterly, installments.

Dividend yield: A dividend payment as a percentage of the share price. For example, a $20 share paying a $1 annual dividend means your dividend yield is 5%.

Capital gains: Appreciation (or increased value) of a stock or investment. This term won't be relevant for most of our income-related discussions, but it's still good to know the distinction.

## The Why

Let's analyze portfolio income respective of the Factors of SCRIMP.

Scalability: not applicable.

Controllability & Regulation: Low. Stocks and dividends depend entirely on the stock market and the company's performance. You have zero control over how a company performs, and bond values fluctuate with interest rates, which you also cannot control.

Investment: Lots of money, no time. To generate enough money from dividends and interest, you typically need a hefty amount of capital.

Marketability: not applicable.

<u>Passivity:</u> High. This income stream literally entails zero work to maintain. Portfolio income is the most passive income stream available.

Within the portfolio income category, you can make passive income via dividends, bonds, and interest, which are the basics. Or you can do something a little more advanced and invest in P2P Lending, MLPs, REITs, and Crowdfunded Real Estate. I'll walk you through how each specific portfolio income stream works, one by one. We'll start with the basic options in this chapter and move onto the advanced options in the next.

## Dividend Income

Generally, when someone like you or me invests in stocks, we are hoping to make money from 1) capital gains and 2) dividends. Capital gains mean that we buy the stock at one price, wait for it to go up, and sell it at a higher price. That's a nice one-time moneymaker, right? If you've ever heard of the term "day-trader," that's what those guys do all day long.

For our goals, we don't want to be working all day long or making a one-time profit. Instead, we are much more interested in making consistent income from dividends. Dividends are paid out regularly, so that's where we get our passive income.

Careful, though: not all stocks pay dividends. The easiest way to tell is by—you guessed it—Googling it! I just Googled "Apple stock" and saw right there in the search results that its dividend yield is 1.31%,[35] so clearly, it does pay a dividend. When I Googled "Netflix stock," I saw no dividend yield; Netflix does not pay a dividend, as of this writing.

Math aficionados, you're up next. Here's a math problem for ya: If you invest $50,000 in Apple stock, with a 1.31% dividend yield, how much will you make in dividends per year?

A.  $6,550
B.  $655
C.  $65.50

The correct answer is B, and I now apologize for anyone who is triggered by the flashback to math class.

The higher the dividend yield → the higher the risk → the higher the reward → the more money you'll make. Buying shares of a brand-new company paying an attractive 8% dividend yield is much riskier than buying shares of Microsoft with its 1.46% dividend yield.[35] Microsoft is an enormous company that's been around a long time with a solid reputation. On the other hand, we know much less about a startup. It's been widely said that over 50% of businesses fail within the first five years.[36] That's part of what makes investing in a startup riskier. With that higher risk does come a higher

*higher reward.* ward. You'll have to decide for yourself e ideal amount of risk you're willing to ke on.

ı a single dividend-yielding stock is that you could lose what you invested if the company goes belly-up. If you were one of the unlucky people invested in Lehman Brothers in 2008, you probably lost a lot of money.

If you're not the type to skydive or bungee jump, then maybe you'd prefer a less risky option for investing in dividends. Enter a dividend-yielding ETF. Instead of putting your money in a single stock, an ETF allows you to invest in all different kinds of stocks at once. Technically, you'll have all sorts of dividend yields, but the ETF will combine everything for you. You can Google "Dividend ETF" to see what I'm talking about. Vanguard offers some great ones (I love Vanguard because they have such low fees. And they didn't even pay me to say that!). Using an ETF instead of a stock helps to spread your money out rather than putting all your eggs in one basket. That's the basic premise of diversification.

A little more math, if you'll allow me. We're going to see how much money you'd need to invest if you are getting a dividend yield of 4%.

If you invest $10,000 you would earn $10,000 x 0.04 = $400 per year or $33 per month. I know, I know, not nearly enough to make a dent. That's why with portfolio investing, you need a large amount of capital. For example, let's try this again, using $250,000 as our investment. With $250,000 invested, you would earn $833 per month. That's better; it covers a big chunk of some people's mortgage or rent payment.

Let's look at it this way: What's the least amount of money you would need to invest to cover all your annual expenses?

First, think of your monthly living expenses. How much money do you need to live on per month? Come up with that number in your mind, and multiply it by 12 to get your annual amount. Now use the following formula to determine how much money you'd need to invest, given a 4% dividend yield:

Initial investment = annual expenses / 0.04

If your annual expenses are $24,000 (I can hear my Bay Area people scoffing at me), you'd need to invest $600,000. If your annual expenses are $50,000, you'd need to invest $1.25 million. Oh perfect! Let me just put that extra mil into the stock market so I can retire. Ha! (Technically, you'd need even more than that to account for taxes.)

The amount you'll need upfront will change depending on the dividend yield. If your annual expenses are $24,000 and your dividend yield is 2%, you'd need to invest $1.2 million. If your dividend yield is 6%, you'd need $400,000. The greater the dividend yield, the less money you'll need to invest.

No matter how you slice it, you need a lot of money to make this work.

People who retire with the goal of living off portfolio income spend forty years of their lives trying to amass an enormous amount of money. Does this sound familiar? It's the Nest Egg Theory! That's not what we're trying to do here. I don't have any idea how to come up with $500K or $1M quickly, so for me and many others, this passive income stream is out of the realm of possibility... at least for now.

That's not to say that it can't be used to supplement some of your other passive income streams. It might be nice to have $500 per month coming in as a truly 100% passive income stream, in addition to the $5,000 per month from other passive income streams.

Another option is transitioning to this particular passive income stream a little bit later. For example, I have my rental properties, and over the next five to ten years, I will build up a decent amount of equity in them. I plan to eventually sell them and reinvest all that capital into an even more passive income stream (like this one). In my opinion, portfolio income is one of the best passive income streams because it is truly passive. Your money is working for you without you lifting a finger.

## Bond Income

And then there were bonds.

Bonds have long been used by retirees and investors to generate income. Again, a bond is a loan, with YOU as the lender. You can loan money to a company, entity, or even the government; in exchange, they pay you interest. That's what a bond is. Cool, right? These interest payments are what would make up your passive income stream.

Here's how it goes down. Let's say you buy a newly-issued bond for $1,000; that is, you agree to lend a company $1,000 of your money in return for interest payments.

Every bond has a coupon rate—and I'm not talking about the kind of coupons that Bed Bath & Beyond give out for 20% off all the time. When it comes to bonds, the coupon rate means the yield.

Let's say your $1,000 bond pays you $10 twice a year (semiannually). So, each year, you take in $20 total in interest payments. That makes your coupon rate 2%. It's similar to dividend yields that we just discussed. The coupon rate tells you what the bond is yielding. Here's the math, just in case you weren't sick of doing algebra:

Coupon rate = annual payment / bond face value

Coupon rate = $20 / $1,000

Coupon rate = 2%

The bond's coupon rate is set when the bond is issued, and it never changes. If the bond in the scenario above is a 30-year bond, you will receive $10 semiannual payments for 30 years.

Let me tell ya a thing or two about bonds. They can feel complicated and confusing. But I need to explain a little bit more so you can understand why they used to be such a popular investment. We're going to talk about the relationship between the bond coupon rate and market interest rates.

How is the coupon rate determined in the first place? When new bonds are issued, the coupon rates offered are typically at or close to current market rates. You know how since 2009 or so, interest rates have been super low? That means that any bonds issued since then were also probably issued at low coupon rates.

Well, in the 1980s, market interest rates were super high. There was a period in the '80s when you couldn't get a home loan without agreeing to a 15% or 16% interest rate. Prevailing market rates at the time were high all around. And coupon rates on bonds were right up there.

Think about a coupon rate of 15% on a bond. A $1,000 bond would yield $150 per year in interest. If you had $50,000 to invest in newly-issued bonds in 1982, you could promise yourself a hefty $7,500 per year income. That's insane!

Then things changed, and rates dropped. Interest rates everywhere have been at an all-time low over the past decade. That's why you stopped seeing bonds being lauded and started hearing stocks and ETFs being celebrated.

Interest rates may very well creep back up again. The point is, when interest rates are low, the coupon rates on newly issued bonds will also be low.

There's a whole lotta other strategies that go into bond prices, interest rates, market rates, and so forth. **What I've talked about so far only applies when you are buying a newly-issued bond and holding onto it until maturity**. If you sell it on the secondary market before maturity, you could lose OR gain money on your investment. I won't get into that because we are only interested in bonds for the regular interest payments and not to buy and sell in the short term.

One other tidbit to keep in mind is inflation. We all live in a world where inflation causes the prices of goods and services to creep up a little each year. But your bond payments won't creep up. Once the coupon rate gets set, it's there to stay. Your $20 payment is your $20 payment. What might be attractive in your first year could feel a lot different in year 15, after years of inflation.

Also, as with dividends, you can invest in a bond ETF. It's a little confusing because an ETF trades like a stock on the market, but it's all invested in bonds. The ETF would pay out its interest via a dividend, just like a stock. It's an option for someone who'd rather invest in a whole bunch of bonds at once instead of hand-selecting them.

## Interest Income

Next up is Plain Jane interest income—the simplest to understand and the easiest to get started.

Think about your average checking or savings account. Chances are, you are paid interest. It might be a minuscule 0.01% interest, but you are paid interest. Your money is working for you.

Nowadays, you can put your money in a high-yield online savings account where it will earn a whole lot more than it would in a checking account. In 2019, many were offering 2.0% or more in interest.

Because rates are so low on things like checking and savings accounts, you need even *more* capital to generate meaningful income. If you put $100,000 into an account earning 2.0% interest per year, you'd make $2,000 per year in interest. While interest income is not viable for most of us, it still counts as a type of passive income.

Another option for generating interest income is a Certificate of Deposit (CD). CDs are sort of like savings accounts you can't touch. You can get a slightly higher interest rate if you agree to hand your money over to a bank and not touch it for X amount of time. That could be six months, one year, two years, or ten years.

In the next chapter, we'll check out some of the more advanced ways to generate portfolio income with P2P Lending, MLPs, REITs, and crowdfunded real estate.

# CHAPTER 14
# *Portfolio Income: The Advanced*

If you wanna turn up the heat on portfolio income, check out the following advanced options.

## Peer-to-Peer Lending

First, we have another interest-generating option: Peer-to-Peer Lending (P2P Lending). P2P Lending is often seen as riskier and more complex than a simple interest-bearing account, so that's why I've lumped it in with the advanced techniques.

The way P2P Lending works is that first, someone needs to borrow money. Instead of going to the bank or another financial institution to borrow it, they crowdsource the loan instead. I'm not talking about asking friends and family to borrow some money. I'm talking about actual, formal, online platforms where lenders and borrowers can come together to facilitate a loan. Anyone can go on to borrow money, and anyone can go on to lend money. The lenders, who are people like you and me, get to select exactly which loans they want to fund. Just like with lending money to a friend, you risk losing your investment if the borrower defaults, but you would typically get a higher interest rate than with a checking or savings account. LendingClub and Prosper are two popular P2P platforms that you can check out if this interests you. They're not offered in every state, but you can check their websites to see if you'd qualify.

## MLPs

I have this rule: Never invest in something you don't understand. Seems pretty reasonable, right?

As an author and finance guru, I also avoid *teaching* anything I don't fully understand. Master Limited Partnerships (MLPs) are not something I have mastered. Still, because they fall into the portfolio income category of all the different passive income streams, I'm bringing them up now. In my time as a financial advisor, I never once used or learned about them. In fact, from my research for *PIAR*, it appears that MLPs are commonly misused and misunderstood. Proceed with caution.

An MLP is a type of business venture and a type of investment that is traded on a stock exchange. I'll explain only how they work at the very highest level. Most MLP businesses operate in the energy, gas, and natural-resource sector. An MLP has a general partner and a limited partner or partners. The limited partners are the investors; people like you and me that would buy units of the MLP on the stock exchange. The investors receive periodic distributions from the MLP; that's your cash flow and passive income.

The benefits of an MLP mostly come in the form of tax advantages, steady and consistent cash distributions, and attractive yields.

If MLPs interest you, please consult a qualified professional that has significant experience with this type of investment specifically. Don't try this at home.

## REITs

I love these babies! REIT, pronounced "reet," stands for Real Estate Investment Trust. They combine two of my favorite types of passive income: rental income and portfolio income. REITs are kind of like a middleman between you and a rental property. The REIT owns a portfolio of income-producing real estate assets which you can invest in, and then you earn a share of the income produced by the properties. Ta-da!

It's nice because you don't have to do all the direct work of finding and investing in properties, finding good tenants and maintaining the buildings. Instead, you are investing in the R⁣ ⁣ ⁣ income.

Congress created this nifty tool in the '60s to give everyone the opportunity to invest in income-producing real estate without needing a ton of capital to buy a property. (One of the few things the government did that, surely, we can ALL agree was awesome!)

Investing in real estate without investing in real estate. Hey, heyyy!

Besides the distinct advantage

*:ITs are a great way to get your feet wet with investing in real estate. You can earn a piece of the pie without actually buying a property.*

of eliminating any work involved in owning a property, REITs also offer diversification, liquidity, and tax advantages.

In terms of diversification, instead of spending all your money on one rental property, REITs pool a bunch of people's money together to maintain a large portfolio of all different types of real estate: single-family, multi-family, residential, commercial, you name it. You might find REITs that focus on residential real estate only, but they're still investing in tons of different residential real estate. It's not just one house or in one city. We're talking a large pool of money here. For you, this means portfolio diversification, which means less financial risk. It's the same reason it's safer to invest in index funds rather than just one individual stock.

REITs are also liquid, unlike traditional real estate investing. If you want to sell, you simply sell your share on the stock exchange. On the other hand, if you own a property, it could take six months to find an agent, list the property, find a buyer, get through inspections, and close. Liquidity is a huge advantage.

As pass-through entities, REITs have a tax advantage, which allows them to distribute even more income to their shareholders. REITs are required to pay out at least 90% of their taxable income as dividends. But, be careful, because depending on how the REIT distributes the dividends, *you* may be taxed at the ordinary income tax rate, which would be a distinct disadvantage. Overall, though, REITs make for an amazing investment option!

## Crowdfunded Real Estate

Fundrise holds the toast when it comes to crowdfunded real estate. Fundrise offers an eREIT, which is similar to a REIT. Think of Fundrise's eREITs as a real estate crowdfunding platform. The main difference is that with an eREIT, you are investing directly into tangible real estate, while with a REIT, you are investing in a corporation that manages a portfolio of real estate. You could experience more transparency with what you are investing in with Fundrise. eREITs are not publicly traded, so they are less liquid than REITs. You can only buy and sell them via Fundrise itself, meaning it can take over a month to redeem your shares and liquidate. For this reason, I would only recommend Fundrise as a long-term investment.

For fun, I tested out the Fundrise platform with a $5,000 investment. The experience was easy, and it was fun to see the 48 specific projects they had invested my money in. Fundrise also sends me notifications when my portfolio has acquired a new project, like a commercial renovation in Los Angeles. After testing the waters for a year, I upped my investment even more.

As of this writing, I'm on track to earn a 7.7% return for the year on the Supplemental Income Plan. The advisory fees are reasonable at only 0.15% per year as of this writing. Other crowdfunding real estate platforms exist besides Fundrise, but Fundrise seems to be the most popular. And by the way, readers, I've got you covered with a discount on advisory fees. You can find it in the FREE *PIAR* Bonus Gift at:
**www.moneyhoneyrachel.com/bonus**.

Whether with REITs, crowdfunded real estate, or any other investment, there's risk. You could lose your money if the REIT doesn't perform well or manage its portfolio well.

I still believe that directly owning rental property is one of the best passive income streams, but for those who aren't quite ready, REITs and crowdfunded real estate are B-E-A-utiful options.

## The Downside

Portfolio income is nearly perfect in the passivity sense. But none of these passive income streams come without risk. And the big risk of portfolio income is losing your capital in a stock market downturn.

The Great Recession of 2008 was devastating for Americans. Even with diversified portfolios, people lost a ton of money, and in some cases are still trying to make up for that, years later.

Also ruinous for the United States was the Dot Com Crash in 2000, the Gulf War Recession in the early '90s, the Iran/Energy Crisis Recession in the early '80s, the Oil Crisis Recession in the mid-'70s... do you see where I'm going with this? The stock market and the US economy are cyclical. Recessions are a matter of *when* not if.

If you keep your money in the stock market long enough, you will lose money on paper. You don't *actually* lose money until you sell, thereby solidifying the loss. Therefore, if you hold onto your investments during a downturn instead of selling, you have a better chance of recompensing your loss.

Because on the sunny side, what goes down must come up. If you've read my book *Money Honey*, you know that investing is only for the long-term. Make sure you have enough time to weather the downs and come back out on top.

## Conclusion

Portfolio income would be my favorite passive income stream... if I had enough money. You see, it's the only stream that's truly 100% passive with no work required, not even in the long-term. Once you invest your money, you sit back and do nothing. You manage no one, you market to no one, you just leave it there. But of course, the safer and easier the investment, the lower the return.

To make enough money to live off, you're easily going to need hundreds of thousands, if not a million dollars. And most people don't have that (myself included.) That's why right now, I don't have much portfolio income. I'm building my passive income streams through other means, and then once I am wealthy enough, I'll probably start switching over to portfolio income. If you can afford it, you won't find an easier way to make money without lifting a finger.

If you want something more hands-on but requiring less money, the next passive income category could be a great fit for you!

# Coin-Operated Machines

## CHAPTER 15

# Small Coin-Ops

## The What

Of all the passive income streams, coin-operated machines are arguably the most unique and fun.

When you think of coin-operated machines, what comes to mind? Maybe you thought of one of the following:

- Vending machines
- ATMs
- Arcade games
- Car washes
- Laundromats
- Slot machines

A coin-operated machine is any machine that automatically provides a good or service in exchange for money. The machine doesn't have to take only literal coins. Many coin-operated machines accept credit cards or ePay, but the name has simply stuck around. All these machines are automated and work only when the user pays. That is, they are "pay-per-use."

For example, an ATM is a type of coin-operated machine that, in exchange for a fee, provides cash money when you need it. An automatic exterior car wash business is a very large coin-operated machine.

So, how does one make money off a coin-operated machine? Let's take a vending machine as an example. Surely you've noticed that a Milky Way bar in your office lobby vending machine is $1.50 more than one at the grocery. Why the extra charge? It's for the convenience factor. They know they can get you because, in a moment of sugar-deprived panic, you'll pay more for the convenience of grabbing one right now rather than getting in your car and driving to the nearest gas station... or at least I will if I'm desperate! (Peanut M&Ms get me.)

The thing is, someone owns these vending machines. Someone is profiting off making snacks and sodas easy for you to buy at a premium cost. The owner might buy sodas for $1.00 each, charge them to you for $2.50 each, and profit.

Vending machines are easy to maintain. The main thing a vending machine owner has to do is keep it stocked, and that can be done with a weekly trip, or it can be outsourced.

Vending works the same way for other types of machines: feminine hygiene products in the women's bathroom, those pressed penny engravers at Disney World, gumball machines, and so on.

Imagine having a whole system of coin-operated machines, like a laundromat, car wash, or slot machines. You set up the space, invest in the machines, and then sit back and let people pay to use them. These businesses are a little more hands-on and will likely need personnel or a security system, but the logic is the same.

## The Why

We'll use the Factors of SCRIMP to weigh the pros and cons of Coin-Operated passive income.

Scalability: Low. Coin-operated machines can only be used physically. When you install an arcade game at a local movie theater, your market is limited to only those at the movie theater. A person living in Asia would not be able to play your arcade game in New Jersey. You are limited by geographic location; this business cannot be scaled online.

Controllability & Regulation: Medium. You have medium control and are subject to business regulations and local laws. With a snack vending machine, you can control where you put it and the price of your product. If you put it in the lobby of a complex that goes out of business, you can opt to move it to a new location. Slot machines would be a lot more regulated, but something like an arcade or car wash would still be mostly subject to your control.

Investment: Depends. If you go with the single machine route, your investment might be a couple of thousand dollars, as well as some time spent. But if you want to open a car wash, that's a whole different ball game, requiring a hefty capital investment and lots of work setting up the business itself.

Marketability: Depends. Buying and installing an ATM next to an already-existing ATM is not your best move, because there is already a supply. You'll need to research to see if there is a demand for what you want to offer. You can't get into the feminine hygiene vending business if every public bathroom in your state already has one.

Passivity: Depends. A single vending machine doesn't require a lot of work, but a coin-operated business like a laundromat will need operational management. In that regard, you could potentially be sliding into the active income category, but it all depends on how you set up the biz.

Based on the Factors of SCRIMP, it seems that single machines (such as buying one or a few snack vending machines) would be a better passive income stream overall than an entire system of machines (such as buying a laundromat or car wash.)

## The How

One by one, I'm going to walk you through the six main types of coin-operated machines.

To make this easier to digest, I'll break these coin-operated machines into two categories. Because I'm super scientific, the first category consists of "small" coin-operated machines: vending machines, ATMs, and arcade games. Small, in this case, means it's not uncommon for just one of these types of machines to be placed in one building. These smaller options are arguably more passive. We'll cover those now, and then in the next chapter, we'll review the second category, which consists of "big" coin-operated machines: car washes, laundromats, and slot machines. These often require much more capital and run the risk of turning into businesses.

## Vending Machines

The basic premise of starting a vending machine business is: do market research, find a location, negotiate an agreement with the owner of the site, buy and install the machine, and begin collecting revenue. Your profit will be the revenue collected minus the cost you paid for the products and any other expenses. Weekly, you or someone you hire will restock and collect the cash and coins.

I love this business model because it's relatively simple and straightforward, and the time requirement will always be the same in the long run. You can see how this will take some time to set up and also some money to buy the machines; but, you can choose to spend a few hours per week restocking, or you can make this totally passive by outsourcing that job and paying someone else to do it.

Location, location, location. Choosing your location is the most important step of starting a vending machine business, and this holds for all coin-operated businesses. Your location could make or break you, so you must do research and choose wisely. An important question to ask yourself is, "For this location, what type of vending machine makes the most sense?" Maybe you find a fantastic lobby space in a huge gymnasium, but is soda really going to sell well there?

While vending machines can dispense tons of different kinds of products (candy, drinks, food, sandwiches, snacks, feminine hygiene products, condoms, and so forth), to keep it simple, I'll talk in terms of drink and snack vending machines from here on out. Just know you can interchange this concept with any other type of vending machine product.

First and foremost, research your state's laws and regulations regarding vending machines. Contact your local chamber of commerce or look up your state's small business regulations online. Understanding what you can and cannot do before you travel too far down this path is crucial.

Once you get clarification, make a list of all possible locations. Think schools, businesses, office complexes, libraries, apartment complexes, gyms, indoor tennis or soccer courts, clubhouses, and so forth.

You'll spend a lot of time upfront prospecting, meaning calling the locations to get more information and pitching them on why it would be in their benefit to work with you and install a vending machine. You will pay the location a commission in return for them "renting" their real estate to you. You can expect to pay the location proprietor anywhere from 10% to 30% of revenue.

Don't buy any equipment or machines until you have zeroed in on your location and are extremely familiar with their needs. You'll want to get a contract with the owner of the building or complex that outlines all of your terms and then have several conversations to understand the most significant want or need in terms of drinks and snacks.

In terms of choosing the products to offer in your food and drink vending machine, you'll want to consider four key areas:

1) Price: Products must be priced competitively; otherwise, they won't sell. If customers can walk next door to the gas station and buy a $1.25 candy bar instead of your $4.00 one, you will probably lose some of your customer base (hint: while doing location research, make sure you know whether there IS a gas station next door.) You can do research and check out vending machine pricing in your area to get an idea of what is common. Estimate conservatively and tweak later.

2) Brand: Offering Coca-Cola or Pepsi is practically a given. Offering some soda from a company that no one has ever heard of is not so great. It's always better to stick with familiar, well-branded products.

3) Mix: What kinds of products will you offer? Chocolate bars? Lemonade? Chips? You'll need to do research and experiment to see what people want the most. This will also help you determine whether you install a drink machine, a snack machine, or both.

4) Nutritional value: This goes along with mix, but in this day and age, there is a definite trend towards healthy eating. Offering more

nutritious snacks like almonds and peanuts, in addition to junk food, can help you attract more customers.

Once you determine your location and machine type, the next steps are to find and buy a machine. Finding a vending machine can be as simple as an online search. You'll be surprised at the options you have just on platforms like eBay, Craigslist, and Facebook Marketplace. UsedVending.com is another great resource.

Vending machines come in different types: bulk machines dispense gumballs and other snacks by the handful and can be a few hundred dollars. Mechanical machines are your typical office vending machine and can be more like a couple of thousand dollars if you purchase new. Electronic machines take it one step further with touch screens and ePay and will cost even more.

Sure, you can buy a brand-new machine with the latest fancy technology, but those can be super expensive, and what are those actually doing for you that an older model can't do? It's almost always better to be more conservative with your money and buy a cheaper used machine. Prepare to spend around $2,000 on a good used vending machine.

Since we're talking money, let's pause here and play out a scenario where we calculate the return on investment (ROI). Let's say you buy a $3,500 machine. Let's say, on average, your products sell for $2.50 each. Most vending machines can hold up to three hundred items. Let's say in an average week you sell fifty items. At $2.50 each, that's $125 in revenue per week. In an average month, you'll generate $500 in sales, and in a year, you'll generate $6,500.

Let's say your products cost you $1.50 each, or $75 per week. Let's say gas and other costs amount to another $15 per week. So, your total costs per week are $90; per year, they are $4,680.

That means you are profiting $6500 - $4680 = $1,820 per year. To calculate your ROI, you divide the annual profit by the initial investment. $1,820 / $3,500 = 52%... that's super high. That's a 52% return. Normally when we are talking about the stock market, we use numbers like 8%, 10%, or 12%. To generate $1,820 off a $3,500 investment is pretty spectacular! See how this can be so exciting?

Obviously, that's a simplified example, and in reality, your numbers will be different. You can work with assumptions you're comfortable with to run some different scenarios. If you find a great location and have competitive prices, chances are you could make a lot more; maybe you are selling 200 items per week, maybe you can charge $2.75 per item. And with multiple vending machines, you can see how the profits can quickly add up.

My friend, before you even get going down this path, you'll want to put together a business plan and financial analysis. Ask yourself things like, if the vending machine costs me X, how many months will it take to make up my investment? It's a numbers game, and if the numbers don't work from the get-go, you *will* lose money. Make sure you understand exactly what it will take from a financial perspective to be successful.

To purchase products for your machine, you can research wholesalers or distributors that sell what you need. Your goal is to buy your products at the lowest price possible. Another great option is to buy from Sam's or Costco, both of which generally offer discounted pricing for bulk purchases.

Once you get going, you can typically expect to "service" your machine(s) once per week. Servicing your machine consists of restocking products, restocking coins, and wiping down the front of the machine. You might not have to restock coins if your machine only accepts credit cards.

I recommend going the DIY route when starting this type of business, meaning learning the ins and outs yourself, buying your own machines, and finding your own locations. It will be the cheapest way to go about it. It will require a time investment since you will have to learn the ropes, and you will need to be strong at selling your product and negotiating. In the end, you are not only learning how to run your own business, but you are also being financially savvy about it.

Another option is to buy an existing vending machine route or business. There may be other vending machine owners in your area who are looking to sell. Assuming it's a profitable business, this can be an easier but costlier way to get your foot in the door. This saves you from having to find and purchase individual machines by yourself and from finding your own locations.

You will find plenty of companies online that exist solely to help people start vending machine businesses. Stay away from them. They will sell you on all sorts of unnecessary things, from software, to the latest tech, to brand new equipment that you don't actually need. If you do a Google search, you'll see plenty of people who have lost money starting a vending machine business. Those people didn't properly research the location and often put up way too much of their own money to begin with. I saw someone post this on a Quora thread, "I lost a bunch of money ($30,000) when I started a vending business in my early 20s. This was partially because I bought new vending machines from a company that specialized in marketing and selling vending machines."[37]

If you are savvy and shrewd, you can make this work, and it can be passive and profitable.

## ATM Vendor

Have you ever been to Churchill Downs in Kentucky and wanted to place a bet on a horse race but didn't have cash? I have. How about only having a card when you show up to your favorite cash-only taco stand? Have you ever paid the $3.00 ATM fee so that you could get cash? Guilty.

Who actually receives that ATM fee? The fee is paid to three parties: the owner of the ATM, the venue owner, and the ATM processor. The ATM owner (that would be you, hypothetically) services the machine and loads it with cash, and in return, receives part of the ATM fee anytime someone withdraws money. The venue owner also receives a portion of the fee since they are allowing you to place the ATM on their premises. They typically receive $0.50 per transaction, but it could be more or less. The ATM processor, which is the company that processes and documents the paperwork and allows the ATM to work, normally is paid a percentage and a flat fee. Let's just say that you pay the ATM processor $0.25 per transaction for simplicity's sake.

The average ATM fee is around $3.00. Your profit is $3.00 minus $0.50 to the venue owner minus $0.25 to the ATM processor... so you're left with $2.25. If six people use the machine in a day, that's $13.50 per day in profit. That's works out to $405 per month! If you consider your time and gas costs and any other costs, let's say you're left with $350. Still... Holy smokes!

The ATM business is very much like a vending machine business: you must think of locations, prospect, research local laws and ordinances, write out your business plan and financial analysis, and so forth.

The main difference is that you're stocking the machine with cash, not sodas and Milky Way bars. If you're stocking the machine with cash, then that's a significant upfront investment. You'll need to fund it yourself with a healthy mix of one-dollar-bills, fives, tens, twenties, and so forth. Every dollar withdrawn will ultimately be returned to you through the customer's bank account, but it's still a cash outlay that you'll need to make in the beginning. You should count on loading the machine with at least $2,000 per week, but the $2,000 is always paid back to you. The *fee* is what you earn as a profit.

The cost of purchasing an ATM can be anywhere from $1,000 to $10,000. Hundreds of online sites sell and lease old and new ATMs, so a quick online search will yield tons of options.

You shouldn't consider the upfront $2,000 cash requirement into your ROI calculations, because that's always refunded back to you, but you should take it into account in calculating how much money you'll need to invest. If you buy a $5,000 machine and fill it with $2,000 in cash, then you'll need $7,000 to get this business going.

Let's take the example above where you make $350 per month in fees. That's $4,200 per year. To calculate your ROI, you'll include all upfront costs except for the $2,000 cash outlay. In this case, you'll divide the annual profit of $4,200 by the cost of the machine of $5,000, which is an 84% ROI. Wow.

Even if you're only making $100 per month in fees ($1,200 per year), with a machine that costs $5,000, that's a 24% return!

It sounds so easy. In reality, the barriers to entry of getting into this business are pretty high because finding a good location is extremely hard. If it were easy, everyone would be doing it, right? Most viable locations already have a vending machine or ATM. The market is saturated. But you can see based on the numbers above how big the payoff can be if you *do* find a spot. You'll need patience. You may search for months before finding what you're looking for. It's sort of like real estate. I've waited nine months before for the ideal property to come around. And once it did, I pounced and made a ton of money. Vending machines and ATMs are pretty similar because it can take a while to find that perfect opportunity.

Just like with the vending machine example, do the math and run the numbers ahead of time. Don't count on the ideal or perfect scenario. Use very conservative estimates so that when it comes down to it, your machine is even more profitable than you thought it would be.

## Arcade Games

Yes, yes, some of you may object, "What could possibly be passive about an arcade business?"

But hear me out. I'm not talking about opening a standalone arcade business. Not only is that not passive, but I'm not convinced there's a market for it anymore. Then again, I'm 27 and haven't frequented an arcade in two decades.

I'm talking about setting up a couple of arcade games in an already-established business. A movie theater a few miles away from me does this; they have a little area in the lobby with a few arcade games. Where else could this work? Perhaps a bowling business, an indoor sports arena, a daycare center, a family restaurant, or anything else that is already oriented around young people's entertainment and fun.

Think of arcade games the way you'd think of vending machines. Where can you install one, two, or five arcade games in an already-established business with good foot traffic that'll get you in front of your target market?

If you can brainstorm and begin having conversations with businesses, then this will work exactly like the vending machines. You'll invest a couple of thousand dollars for the equipment and share any revenue with the owner of the location. Each week, you'll service the machines by collecting money and wiping them down.

Like the other coin-operated machines, this requires a lot of upfront research and time. Will people actually play on them? What games are the most popular? How do you ensure your machines or games don't become outdated? How much do you charge?

My explanations are getting shorter because in general, coin-operated machines all work the same way. If you understand how to operate one type of coin-operated machine, you understand how to operate all of them.

A financial analysis and ROI calculation can be done for arcades as well. Calculate how many games will be played each day and at what price, using very conservative estimates. Estimate your total initial investment and ongoing costs. See if the numbers work.

On the whole, owning one or two small coin-operated machines likely won't enable you to retire. But owning a bunch of them might, and pairing them with other passive income streams certainly will!

# CHAPTER 16

## Big Coin-Ops

We are ready to move onto the "big" coin-operated machines: car washes, laundromats, and slot machines. These often require much more capital and run the risk of turning into businesses, but they can still be passive.

### Car Wash

*Breaking Bad*, anyone? Channel your inner Walter White and start a car wash... but follow the law.

A car wash is an enormous undertaking. It takes a lot of money, it's riskier in terms of liability and money, and it's difficult to find a location. Before I totally scare you off, it can be a fantastic option for someone who does have the money, has identified a market need, and is business-savvy. If you set up *one* successful car wash, it could generate enough passive income to be fully retired. Most other ideas in this book will need to be multiplied or done in conjunction with another passive income stream to get to that $10,000 per month mark.

Just like the vending machines and ATMs, car washes aren't automatically successful. You can't plop one down anywhere and expect to make a ton of money. It's all about location, location, location.

Research first. Drive around and see where other car washes are placed and whether they stay busy all day or not. Learn where everyone tends to go after a snowy or rainy day when cars are dirty. Determine what would be the #1 most desirable location for a new car wash in your city.

Not only will you research your location, but you'll research local laws and regulations, insurance needs, and permits and licenses.

Opening a car wash requires an enormous capital investment. Not only do you have to purchase or rent land, but you also have to invest in the car wash itself, which will be tens of thousands of dollars.

Since we are focusing on passive income streams, you'll want to open a fully automatic car wash. These are the ones where a driver can pull up, pay through their window at a little machine, pull through the car wash, and be done. These businesses require no employees and less effort on the owner's part. You'll frequently see these next to grocery stores and gas stations.

A large business like this requires a certain amount of ongoing marketing. How will people hear about your car wash? Why would they go there? How will you get the word out? You will want to consider a grand opening of some sort. You'll need to build a customer base through advertising.

*a single cent without completely understanding the total initial cost, ongoing costs, and expected profits.*

To estimate all this, you can work with: A) a commercial realtor to find land, B) construction companies to understand quotes for building anything out, and C) local equipment distributors to compare equipment pricing. You can expect to invest anywhere from $40,000 to $100,000 for a one-bay automatic car wash. The International Carwash Association is a great resource for understanding everything from car wash trends to reputable suppliers.

It's worth repeating yet again: any of these ventures require a full, detailed business plan and financial analysis before pursuing them. You should not invest a single cent without completely understanding the total initial cost, ongoing costs, and expected profits. You stand to lose a lot of money if you don't.

A car wash, in particular, can be a full-blown business. It takes a significant time *and* capital investment. There's nothing passive about it for the first six to twelve months during Stage 1. As we already know, passive income streams do require upfront investment; once you get them going, *then* they become passive. But, if you do the car wash right, then it can become pretty passive after it gets going. Ongoing work could include marketing and restocking soaps and supplies for your machines, and that can all be outsourced.

## Laundromat

A couple of years ago, I seriously considered opening a laundromat. My eyes hadn't yet been opened to all the different types of passive income specifically, but I somehow came across the idea of a laundromat and was very interested.

A laundromat can be as passive as you make it. You can set up the business so that anyone can enter and use the machines with pay-per-use. You can install a security system. You can hire an onsite employee. Ideally, you'd set it up and then sit back and collect money. Operating that passively will likely require both an upfront time and capital investment as well as hired help so that you don't physically have to be there.

A laundromat is similar to a car wash in terms of initial setup and investment. You'll need to find land, a building, and equipment. Commercial laundry is expensive; outfitting an entire building with thirty or more machines is no small feat.

You can start from scratch and build your own laundromat, or you can purchase an existing business. The startup cost will vary enormously depending on the size, equipment, location, and more. The best range I can give you is anywhere from $200,000 to $500,000. Then you have ongoing costs: payroll, insurance, lease costs, utilities, and supplies. And if you have that much money, why not just go with portfolio income? (That's what I would do!)

You can profit in several ways: pay-per-use income from the laundry machines themselves, charging for supplies like detergent and dryer sheets, charging fees if customers opt to use their credit or debit cards instead of paying with coins, and so forth. You can even combine coin-operated machine businesses by installing a vending machine or ATM in your laundromat. You can hire an employee and offer an onsite folding service for a fee. The ideas are endless.

An owner who runs his or her store well (or who has a good manager to do so), lands a profitable location, is good at marketing, and keeps things serviced and clean, could enjoy profit margins of 35%. That means that if your revenues are $30,000 a month, you profit 35% of that, or $10,500, with the other $19,500 going towards expenses.

The opposite type of owner could be in the hole and lose money each month. The success of your business depends on the research you do, your business plan, and, most importantly, YOU. Opening a car wash or a laundromat is betting on yourself and your abilities more than anything else.

For those who don't have a ton of money or are curious about doing this on a smaller scale, think of the people who install laundry machines in dormitories... there's an idea! No need to purchase land or the building—just the equipment. These laundry owners might spend $2,000 on a washer and dryer. If they charge $1.50 per use (so $3.00 to both wash and dry), and the students in the dorm do an average of three loads per day, that's $9 per day. That works out to $270 a month and over $3,000 per year! Of course, you have to subtract your ongoing expenses, which could include a share of the utility bills and whatever fees you are paying to the college, but that's still an incredible ROI.

Typically, college dorms already have agreements with laundry companies or corporations, but you can be creative. You can reach out to local landlords. You can opt to install a few laundry machines in an apartment complex, dorm, or gym. It wouldn't hurt to start making a massive list of businesses and multi-family properties in your area and start calling around. You can offer landlords a share of the profits or a rental rate in return for them allowing you to put your laundry machines in their building. Same for gyms, indoor pools, or anything else that might require a shower and change of clothes.

Setting up a couple of laundry machines in an already-operating business would cost you way less—maybe a few thousand dollars. It would be super passive; all you'd have to do is go by (or hire someone to go by) to collect the coins. Or avoid that altogether by purchasing machines that accept credit cards. You can see how this can turn out to be one of the most passive coin-operated machines.

How passive a laundromat is depends on the way you set up the business. It's harder than you think to set it up to ultimately be hands-off, so be careful with this one! You don't want to slide into active income.

## Slot Machines

First of all, slot machines aren't even legal in every state in the US and, even where they are, they are subject to extreme scrutiny and legal requirements. You must be properly licensed, which can take years. If this interests you at all, I strongly suggest working with an attorney to ensure you aren't unintentionally doing anything illegal.

Now that that fun disclaimer is over with, a slot machine business is in many ways similar to the other coin-operated machines. They are highly location-dependent, require a lot of market research, and will definitely need an upfront business plan and financial analysis. Like arcade games, the servicing needs for slot machines are low, and generally, you only need to make your rounds to collect money.

Since gambling is such a tricky biz, and one that I have no personal experience with, I'll stop there. You'll need to consider tons of important regulations, such as being able to limit usage to customers that are at least 21 years of age. You may have to split part of your profit with the state and also the venue owner.

If this idea interests you, I'd recommend doing research and seeking out a slot machine owner that can serve as a mentor to you.

## Conclusion

The coin-operated ideas are endless. I've touched on the main ones, but you'll see coin-operated machines everywhere. What about those bikes or electric scooters for rent that you see in many cities today? Take the company Bird; Bird has an inventory of thousands of scooters that sit in cities all over the US. If you see a Bird scooter sitting on a sidewalk, all you have to do is download the app to pay, and then you activate the scooter and ride it wherever you want to go. It's a genius idea and allows people to get around downtown areas easily. Bird scooters are coin-operated machines! If you think of and create something like that, you'd be set for life.

A coin-operated passive income stream, like with any other type of business, can either make you money or lose you money. Any investment has risk. Our goal with this passive income stream is to reduce the risk as much as possible so that we are successful in creating this income for ourselves.

As you may have noticed as you were reading, you can do lots to lower your risk. First, conduct so much market research that you are left feeling absolutely no "what ifs," "buts," or hesitations.

Run the numbers. Before you do anything, you should have several projections of exactly how profitable your business would be, assuming X, Y, and Z. You should know beforehand how much you'll make each month and what your risks and opportunities are. Be conservative in all of your estimates. Run a worst-case scenario and ask yourself, "If that's what the profits ended up looking like, would I regret this?"

Ensure you are compliant. Research local laws, regulations, business ordinances, permits, licenses, insurance, and zoning.

Be tenacious and committed. Your coin-operated business is only as good as you are. Run it like a professional, don't be lazy, and think in terms of the long run. If you pull this off, it can be a very unique, fun, and enduring passive income stream. I mean, who wouldn't want to make money off stuff like arcades and gumball vending machines? You'd be making a lot of people's lives happier!

So far, we've discussed royalties, which require lots of time and little to no money; and portfolio income, which requires lots of money and no time. Coin-operated machines fall somewhere in the middle. You'll need to invest some time and likely at least a couple thousand dollars of capital. This type of passive income stream can be super amusing, lucrative, and as hands-off as you want to make it.

On deck, we have another interesting and fun passive income stream requiring a decent time investment...

# SECTION FIVE:

# Ads and E-commerce

# CHAPTER 17

# "A" is for Ads & Affiliates

## The What

This chapter includes some unique passive income streams centered around advertising, e-commerce, and dropshipping.

Advertising is a subtle part of everyday life. Every time you buy something, click on a link, or watch videos online, you are witnessing advertising. Affiliate links pass traffic to a product where one can earn a commission for sales. Google gets paid anytime someone places a Sponsored Ad to appear at the top of search results. People hosting podcasts make money from ads featured throughout the podcast. YouTubers make money if an advertiser wants to pay them to place their ad. Not all of these are easy or make sense for everyone, but I'll show you which ones you can take advantage of.

E-commerce is the word used for any online commercial transaction. Within the large e-commerce category, we will specifically discuss the magic of dropshipping, which is slightly reminiscent of PODs in Chapter 9 on royalties. With dropshipping, you generally have a physical product sold through an online interface. The magic happens in that you don't carry an inventory. You purchase or store items with a third party and ship them directly from the third party to the customer. Dropshipping makes e-commerce simple, fluid, and passive.

## The Why

Let's take a look at the Factors of SCRIMP when it comes to ads and e-commerce.

Scalability: High, since ads and e-commerce are done online.

Controllability & Regulation: Low. You are dependent on advertisers, online platforms that you likely don't own, and third-party vendors.

Investment: Expect a decent time investment and sometimes a small capital investment.

Marketability: Depends. If you find a unique product that fills a need with low competition, it will be very marketable.

Passivity: Both advertising and dropshipping can be passive in certain circumstances.

## The How

We can divide this passive income category into three main areas: Affiliate Marketing, Ads, and Dropshipping. First, I'll expand on affiliate marketing and ads: what they are, how they work, and how you can get started. In the next chapter, we'll inspect dropshipping.

## Affiliate Marketing

Affiliate marketing has quickly become popular. Here's a breakdown of how it works: let's say I have a group I interact with a lot on Facebook, where we recommend cute clothing items to each other. There's an adorable summer dress I saw online that I want to share. And because I have an agreement with the company, I use a special link called an affiliate link to post it and share it with my friends. If one of my friends purchases the product through my link, then I get paid a very small piece of revenue (normally just a few cents.)

Affiliate marketing gets a bad rap because links are often posted with zero disclosure of what they are and how they work. That can feel sneaky, unfair, and unethical to people who purchase through the link and don't realize someone is making a piece of the pie off of that purchase. If people can't tell whether someone online is posting a product because they really love it or because they're trying to make money from being an affiliate, that's a problem.

*\ffiliate marketing gets a bad rap because links are often posted with zero disclosure of what they are and how they work. That can feel sneaky, unfair, and unethical...*

You can see how a celebrity who posts an affiliate link to her 2,000,000 followers can make a quick buck this way. More and more, influencers and celebrities are being required to disclose when they are being paid to post something. In fact, social media platforms and websites have had to crack down on the usage of these links. Users online are getting savvier in spotting these links, too. You should always clearly disclose that you will make money if someone chooses to buy something through your link. Here's a clue: check out the Federal Trade Commission's Enforcement Guide to make certain you're being honest, transparent, and NOT misleading in the way you post affiliate links.

Affiliate marketing works well with someone who already has a platform, following, or a large online network. A woman with a blog about shoes could post affiliate links for shoes and rake in money for recommending a product that isn't even hers! It's a pretty nifty form of advertising.

Also, anyone can start doing it. You don't need a following. You don't even need a website or blog. Anyone with a social media account can post affiliate links for his or her friends and family to use.

One of my creative friends started a Facebook group to do just this! She finds deals on Amazon, and through something called Amazon Associates, she shares the deals with her group. Anytime someone buys something, she makes a little moolah.

I've already mentioned Amazon's specific program for affiliate marketing called Amazon Associates. You can look into several other websites: ShareASale, Affiliate Window (AWIN), and MaxBounty. If you're ever unsure of how to find an affiliate link, you can simply think of the product you want to promote and do a Google search for "affiliate program for [insert product or brand]" and see what comes up.

And how passive is this really? Once you've built up a following and you're making good money, how do you keep it going without being actively involved in the business? This is a little trickier, and this particular idea might get me in trouble with some people for not being passive enough—fair enough. The easy answer is to hire someone to continue to find and post links, market to your following, and promote your blog or website. But how will they know how to continue to run your platform the way you were doing it? They can't capture your specific engaging personality and voice. But if you want it to be passive, then you'll need to have a game plan to hire some writers and contributors down the road.

Another idea is to come up with a system for pre-planning and scheduling social media posts. You can block time and spend a few hours this week drafting some posts with links to be sent out on certain days. If that's feasible, and if you're spending ten hours per month to maintain profits, I'd argue that's pretty passive.

You likely won't see those numbers right away. You might spend 18 months working thirty hours per month and generating $300 per month before this really starts to take off for you. It will take a lot of people buying products through your links to generate meaningful revenue. And building a large following will take time: months, possibly years. Think of this particular passive income stream as requiring an upfront time (not capital) investment.

## Advertising

Another way to generate passive income is by placing ads. Advertising requires an even larger, more engaged following than does affiliate marketing. That's because placing ads means that you need to have somewhere to put them, such as a blog or a website. Not just anyone on social media can decide to start generating ad revenue.

If you already have a platform or following, then I'll assume you already understand things like keywords, driving traffic to your site, and search engine optimization (SEO). The next step is to monetize your platform by getting paid to advertise.

Ads literally come in all shapes and sizes, and you'll need to determine the best type. Some ads can be colorful banners across your page, some can be small text ads within your content, or some can be medium-size pictures on the side of your page. Be careful not to clutter your page with too many ads, since that's a huge turnoff for viewers.

Google is one of the largest advertising companies in existence. Luckily for you, they make it easy for bloggers and websites to collaborate with them via Google AdSense. Google Adsense is a program that lets web owners and bloggers display ads on their websites and get paid. Google finds the advertisers for you and tries to pair you with ads that are already related to your keywords. What does this mean for you? A simple, hands-off process.

Google isn't the only one that will hook you up with ads. You can also check out infolinks, media.net, Chitika, and BuySellAds.

Normally, you're paid based on the number of clicks, number of sales, or number of views. Affiliate marketing, for example, only pays when someone clicks on your link and buys it (so, number of sales). Other advertisements pay based on any of the three methods.

For example, let's say you have a blog that gets one hundred thousand visitors per month. (Hint: that's a lot, and that takes a long time to build.) Let's say you can expect 1% of those visitors to click on a link or ad on your site... that's a thousand people. If that ad pays $0.01 per click, that's $10. If the ad pays $1.00 per click (too high to be very likely), then that's $1,000. You can see how it will take a large platform and many ads to generate substantial income. That's why this particular passive income stream of advertising should only be pursued by readers who already have a significant following.

The tricky part here, again, is turning this into a passive stream. The activity of blogging and creating content for a website is not passive at all. That takes a ton of work. But if you build it up enough and have strong momentum to carry you forward, can you begin to outsource or reduce the time you spend on the business so it can start becoming passive? To help you envision this possibility, check out the case studies below.

## Two Case Studies: Chhavi Agarwal & Bobby Hoyt

Chhavi Agarwal is the founder of Mrs. Daaku Studio, a blog about making money online and working from home. Chhavi is a lawyer-turned-blogger based in India.

Chhavi: *[As a lawyer,] I had crazy work hours, which left me no time to focus on family, hobbies, or travel. This is what inspired me to work towards a location-independent life. The idea of passive income is addicting!*

Chhavi started her blog, Mrs. Daaku Studio, in mid-2018. Her initial goal was to make $100 and get ten thousand page views. Not only did she quickly achieve that, but she currently earns $3,000 per month consistently from Mrs. Daaku Studio, just one year later. Her long-term goal is to grow her income so that she and her husband can travel without having to work. She sees herself working around ten hours per week and making $10,000 per month.

Chhavi notes that starting her blog was not passive in the beginning: *Blogging takes time, and you will have to put in hours of work before you see any results. But after a couple of years, most things will run passively. You can make money while you sleep! I know bloggers that make upwards of $100,000 per month. The potential is unbelievable!*

> " *and you will have to put in hours of work before you see any results. But after a couple of years, most things will run passively... The potential is unbelievable!* "
>
> -Chhavi Agarwal

Chhavi's advice to anyone pursuing this path? Start now. She also recommends taking a course, something she didn't do, and then felt was a mistake. Taking a course from a pro ensures that you are doing all the right things from the very beginning.

Chhavi: *Passive income and blogging is real. Read about it and try it out.*

Check out Chhavi's blog at www.mrsdaakustudio.com. You can also follow her on social media.

Facebook: www.facebook.com/mrsdaakustudio

Instagram: www.instagram.com/mrs_daaku

Twitter: www.twitter.com/Mrs_Daaku

Also, remember "Millennial Money Man" Bobby Hoyt from Chapter 10 on online courses? In addition to online courses, Bobby has a blog and website. He earns $1,000+ per month from ads from his website, www.millennialmoneyman.com, completely ~~~~~~~~~

Bobby says: *Since I created most of the content that actually generates the revenue months ago, this feels totally passive. The money is deposited into my bank account every month.*

Now, he has teams and assistants in place to continue generating content to maintain revenue. Ad revenue *can* be passive; it just takes a lot of upfront time.

I've touched on the two big areas of passive advertising income, but don't limit yourself to affiliate marketing or placing ads on your website. Begin to observe the world around you. Where else are you noticing advertisements? Do you hear them in the podcast you listen to? Do you have a podcast, or could you start a podcast? Do you see them in the YouTube videos you watch? Do you enjoy making videos, or do you have a YouTube channel? What about apps on your Smartphone? Do you have an app idea that you can offer for free and generate revenue from advertisements? The possibilities are endless!

*Since I created most of the content... months ago, this feels totally passive. The money is deposited into my bank account every month.*

# CHAPTER 18

# Do's & Don'ts of Dropshipping

I first learned about dropshipping from MJ DeMarco's book *The Millionaire Fastlane*. 10 out of 10, do recommend.

Shopify is a great resource for all things dropshipping, and they give a fabulous rundown of what dropshipping is on their website:

> *Dropshipping is a retail fulfillment method where a store doesn't keep the products it sells in stock. Instead, when a store sells a product, it purchases the item from a third party and has it shipped directly to the customer. As a result, the merchant never sees or handles the product.*
>
> *The biggest difference between dropshipping and the standard retail model is that the selling merchant doesn't stock or own inventory. Instead, the merchant purchases inventory as needed from a third party—usually a wholesaler or manufacturer—to fulfill orders.*[38]

Traditionally, there are four parties involved in the production and sale of a product:

- Consumer: this is the final person that buys the product for consumption. When you buy jeans at Gap, you're a consumer. When you buy wrapping paper from Amazon, you're a consumer.
- Retailer: This is the entity that sells to the consumer. In the examples above, Gap and Amazon are retailers.
- Wholesaler or Distributor: To purchase products from manufacturers, retailers typically work through a middleman called a wholesaler or distributor. These parties are more obscure.
- Manufacturer: This is the entity that actually creates the product. Products in America are often made in China or other places overseas.

Essentially, the model for selling a product looks like this:

*Manufacturer* → *Wholesaler* → *Retailer* → *Consumer*

Working with a dropshipper cuts out at least one or two of the middlemen. When you get into this business, your job is to get the consumer to buy the product. Then, if you can find a manufacturer that will dropship, you can have them send the product directly to the consumer once you make a sale. You are responsible for facilitating the sale, and the manufacturer does the rest:

*Dropshipping manufacturer* → *Consumer*

More often, people end up working with a dropshipping wholesaler or a dropshipping distributor, thereby cutting out the retailer:

*Manufacturer* → *Dropshipping wholesaler* → *Consumer*

Dropshipping enables you to sell products without having to invest thousands of dollars in inventory. Think back to POD shirts in Chapter 9; it's the same brilliant concept. One might argue that POD is technically a form of dropshipping, in fact! With dropshipping, it's not until you've made the sale and the consumer pays that you have to purchase the product to send to them.

Since you're not dealing with physical inventory, you don't have to handle all those pesky tasks like packing and shipping, finding warehouse or storage space for your product, managing inventory levels, processing returns, dealing with many overhead costs, and a lot more.

Not only does that eliminate the upfront capital investment, but it also greatly reduces your *risk*. You won't be betting thousands of dollars of your own money on a product that may not ever sell. That's not to say that building this passive income stream requires zero capital. Stage 1 will require time and potentially some money to build a website, even if you use Shopify. Unless you have software and coding skills, plan on spending some cha vital a good-looking website is.

*you to sell products without having to invest thousands of dollars in inventory.*

Competition is fierce in today's dropshipping world. The most difficult piece of the puzzle is finding a winning product to sell.

There are two ways you can sell products with dropshipping:

1) Sell existing products from a dropshipping wholesaler

2) Invent your own product and have it manufactured and dropshipped

Understanding the difference is crucial because the first, more traditional way to dropship is less passive—and some would say not passive at all. But you'll need to know how that works to understand why the second way is arguably more passive and profitable.

## Selling existing products from a dropshipping wholesaler

This first method is what most dropshippers do. They find, market, and sell stuff that already exists.

People do this by marketing products offered by wholesalers. Working with wholesalers offers both advantages and disadvantages. It's nice not to handle inventory, but that means you must depend on the wholesaler to manage stock and shipping, which means you have relatively low control. Other people can make errors, but ultimately, it's your business, and you need to be responsible for them.

Let's assume a few variables so we can see how this works. Let's say you sell products on a website that attracts one thousand visitors per month. We'll assume your conversion rate, meaning the number of visitors that actually buys one of your products, is 2%. So out of one thousand visitors per month, twenty people will place an order. If your average order value is $50, and your profit margin is 20%, then your average profit is $10 per item. If you make $10 per item on twenty items, that's $200 per month. Your monthly visitors, conversion rate, average order value, and profit margin could all be more or less, but that's how to project how much you might make.

Historically, it's been cheap for wholesalers to source products from China, but all that depends on the current trade deals that the US has with other countries. Recently, some of those profits have been eaten away, making dropshipping a game of large volume. It'll take lots of sales at a low profit margin to make meaningful money.

Also, because dropshipping has such low startup costs and there's a lot of competition, people who get into this business will often drop their prices as low as possible to gain traction. That means you must also drop prices in order to compete, resulting in lower profits.

Being able to start a dropshipping business all depends on finding an already-existing product people want or need or that solves a problem. That could be something as simple as a tote bag, a nice piece of jewelry, or a complex security camera system.

Being able to start a *passive* dropshipping business all depends on finding a unique product that has *long-term marketability*. Often dropshippers have success pouncing on the hottest new thing. If that is the case for you, you are constantly going to be researching the latest trends... sort of like a musician that has to keep dropping new songs. And guess what? Not passive, my friend.

If—and this is a big if—you hit a gold mine and find lasting, selling products you're able to corner the market on, this type of dropshipping can be passive.

Once you have a product in mind, you can do market research. Make sure it is viable, test it out with real people, see what your competition is, and figure out how it should be priced. From there, you would find a wholesaler that will work for you. A few ways to find a dropshipping wholesaler include looking online, purchasing a supplier directory, and contacting manufacturers for recommendations. Again, do your research. Do they offer fraud protection? Do they insure orders? Are they credible? Do they have testimonials they can offer you? Do they have good reviews?

Next: where do you sell your product? You can do dropshipping with eBay, with Amazon, and especially with Shopify, which is *the* go-to dropshipping platform. Shopify has a service called Oberlo that will guide you through setting up your entire business. They make it look like the easiest thing ever; their entire website and setup blow my mind. If nothing else, it's a great place to start to learn more about how the business works and get some questions answered.

You can also get into dropshipping by purchasing an existing dropshipping business. I recently read online about someone who bought a Shopify store for $8,000, improved upon it, and now generates $2,500 in profit with little to no work.[39] It's an interesting option if you have the money and do your homework.

So yes, I'll get some kickback from dropshippers or people familiar with the business who agree that *dropshipping is not passive, ma'am!* The opportunities within the conventional dropshipping strategies outlined above are growing smaller each year. The market is becoming saturated, which makes it difficult to set up a *passive* dropshipping business this way. A much better use of your time could be inventing and creating your own product to dropship.

## Inventing your own product and having it manufactured and dropshipped

If it takes a unique product with long-term marketability to set up a passive dropshipping business, then why not invent your own product?

Some might argue that inventing your own unique product is better or worse, harder or easier, than traditional dropshipping. If you invent a product, you must license it, prototype it, and find a manufacturer that can produce the product as sales come in—a manufacturing process called "Made to Order." This process is difficult and costs more money. Plus, how would you think of something that doesn't already exist?

If you don't deem yourself creative or an inventor, find someone who is. Pick his or her brain. Maybe it will help spark ideas, or maybe you can offer to partner with them and help them turn their ideas into reality. Think about the things that bother you in daily life and how you could fix them. Ladies, if the water dripping down your arms and elbows annoys you when you wash your face at night, what new product could solve that problem? (Take my money!)

For example, I recently attended a dinner gathering where I talked to a lovely couple. About 15 years ago, Joyce Miller asked her husband Bill to make her a cooktop cover. She hated the wasted surface area on her island, and she wanted a simple flat cooktop cover that would be both aesthetically pleasing and give her additional working counter space. Bill, an engineer by trade, put something together for her, and then when they hosted a dinner party, their guests raved about how much they liked it. They all wanted one too! Joyce and Bill began taking orders. They found a local contract manufacturer that could make the cooktop covers and opened biz. To date, they've made over $500,000 in revenue! (You can check out their unique product at www.cooktopcover.com.)

Thinking of something new that no one else has thought of is very difficult but will likely be the most fruitful. Improving a product that already exists will also work.

This would work the same way as traditional dropshipping except that you have control over the unique product, because hey, you invented it. To set up shop, you will have to do one of two things:

1) Find a made-to-order manufacturer that also dropships
2) Find a manufacturer and a dropshipping wholesaler willing to work with you and your product

Dropshipping success centers around having an awesome, marketable product that fills a need. Then it's about finding someone who can produce or supply it and setting up your online platform to generate sales.

## Conclusion

Affiliate marketing, advertising, and dropshipping are excellent passive income stream ideas for anyone who already has a platform or for anyone who's Internet-savvy and excited about the thought of venturing into the world of e-commerce. Like some of the other income streams, it will be as passive as you make it. You must intentionally create ad or e-commerce revenue that is designed to be fully outsourced. It requires time to build up and get the momentum going, but the opportunity to make a consistent stream of income with little work is exciting. The goal eventually would be to hire a social media manager or assistant who can handle most aspects of the business so that it can be as passive as possible.

I have one more passive income category to introduce you to, and luckily for you, I've saved the best for last. Keep reading to learn about my favorite passive income stream and why I think everyone should pursue it!

# SECTION SIX
# Rental Income

# CHAPTER 19

# Rental Income—It's for Everyone

## The What

Finally! We made it to my favorite type of passive income: rental income.

Rental income is generated when you own property and rent it out. The most common type of rental income is with a rental property—a house, triplex, apartment building, or office building that you own and lease to tenants. You buy the property, pay the mortgage and other expenses, and then rent it out at a rate that is high enough to generate acceptable, profitable cash flow.

You can also creatively generate rental income by renting out storage space, a spare bedroom, your car for ad space (really), or parking space.

These ideas all fall into the direct rental income category. You can *indirectly* generate rental income through REITs or platforms like

Fundrise, which we already discussed in the portfolio income chapter. I'll still touch on indirect rental income a little and talk about why I think direct rental income is better.

## The Why

Let's analyze rental income based on the Factors of SCRIMP. We will specifically consider direct, residential real estate for this exercise.

Scalability: Low. Just like with coin-operated machines, rental income is a physical thing. You have to own physical property. That may limit you to your geographic area or not, but it's pretty difficult to go from one single-family home to 10,000 rental units quickly. Rental income is not very scalable.

Controllability & Regulation: Medium. You are in full control of your property, subject to laws. For example, you can't violate local code or kick a non-paying tenant out onto the street. Tenants are a big liability. You can't control how they act, if they pay rent, or how they treat the property.

Investment: Depends. Most people think that buying a rental property requires a ton of cash, but that's not necessarily true. You can either save up thousands of dollars to put down on a rental property, or you can find ways around that. Investing in real estate also requires upfront time in terms of finding a property, buying a property, renovating, and finding good tenants.

*a full-time landlord. Passive rental income is dependent on having a property manager.*

Marketability: If your rental property is competitive (both in terms of pricing and the condition of the unit), it will rent.

Passivity: High... Assuming you have a property manager, and that's a VERY important assumption. The goal of generating rental income is to hire a property manager so that you don't have to manage your rentals actively. With a property manager, rental income is very passive. Without it, you could be a full-time landlord, and that's no bueno.

## Indirect vs. Direct

First, a brief review of the merits of REITs and crowdsourced real estate, both of which provide indirect rental income. Please refer back to Chapter 14 on portfolio income for an explanation of what they are and how they work.

Although these indirect investments belong to portfolio income, they are worth comparing to actual, physical real estate investing.

First, indirect rental income can have a lower startup cost. Investing the minimum amount into a REIT or Fundrise (with minimums as low as $1,000) is much easier than saving enough money for a down payment on a rental property.

Also, your money is better diversified with indirect real estate investing. You can invest a little money into lots of different properties instead of a lot of money into a few properties. That lower risk translates to lower reward.

You have less control over indirect since you are not actively managing the rentals; you are simply an investor fronting the money. On the other hand, indirect rental income is truly passive and requires no management or time investment, whereas direct rental income requires a little work without a property manager and even less work with a property manager.

Rental income, whether direct or indirect, entails plenty of pros and cons all around. I personally still believe direct rental income takes the cake, and I'll explain why. Others, however, will strongly feel that indirect is much better for his or her personal situation, and that's awesome, too! I think it's important to be invested in real estate one way or another.

## The How

Now we'll move onto direct rental income, which involves actually owning and renting property. Direct rental income comes in all shapes and sizes. You can have short-term rentals using Airbnb or VRBO that are rented out for a few days or weeks at a time. You can also rent space, such as your garage for storage or even your car for ad space. If you think really big, you can buy things like parking garages and warehouses and rent out those spaces. And then you have your traditional, long-term rental property investing, which can be either residential (think a single-family house) or commercial (think an office building that would be leased to business owners or companies.)

Let's take it one-by-one and talk through the logistics.

Using Airbnb or renting out vacation homes works exactly like traditional rental property investing, it's just for a shorter time than a conventional one-year lease. Short-term rentals have become quite regulated, and many cities now require permits to operate as an Airbnb. The cool thing is, as long as you have the required permits, you buy in the correct zones, and you follow your local regulations, anyone that owns property can list it on Airbnb. You don't even have to list your whole house. You could offer a spare bedroom on the weekends, or you could offer a week at your vacation home when you know you won't be there.

Because of the shorter-term lease, these rentals require more work. Airbnbs are professionally cleaned between guests, and you normally have to provide all supplies—from bedsheets to kitchen utensils to toilet paper. The upside is that more work typically means more profit.

Generally, with short-term rentals, people use a platform like VRBO or Airbnb to list their property, and the platform supports them in all ways, from selecting a qualified guest to enforcing payment. That can make things simpler and easier than creating your own lease documents and agreements.

Renting space is another creative passive income idea. People need storage for their belongings. Do you have a garage while your neighbor doesn't? Maybe they'd be interested in paying you $40 per month for the privilege of parking their car in your garage in the winter. Do you have a basement, large closet, or extra storage space? Maybe someone would rather pay you $50 per month to rent your storage space instead of $125 per month for a small storage container at a storage facility. There's a website called "Neighbor: The Airbnb of Storage." They help match you with people who need storage space. And readers, if you'd like to earn a bonus when your space rents out, I've got you covered with a special sign-up link that's included in the *free PIAR* Bonus Gift—download it at **www.moneyhoneyrachel.com/bonus.**

Speaking of storage facilities... hello?! A storage facility takes this passive income idea to another level. Lots of money in this! Same with buying and renting out a parking garage. With any idea in this book, think about how you can multiply it by 100 to get the most bang for your buck.

You can even get paid to put advertisements on your car. Just Google "How to rent your car for ad space" or something along those lines. Be careful of the fake car ad companies that scam people. You shouldn't be asked to pay anything up front to apply. As good as this one sounds, don't hold your breath; these companies normally only want to pay people who live in a big city and drive a lot.

The point is, there are lots of ways to make rental income. You just have to look for them.

The most typical type of rental income is from traditional commercial or residential investing. Commercial real estate includes office buildings, warehouses, and shopping malls. If you own something like that, you can lease it out to business owners that need a place to run their business or open their store. The reason I'm not going to go into much detail is that if you think it takes a lot of money to buy a single-family investment property, that's nothing compared to how much it costs to buy an entire office complex, for Pete's sake. Buildings that big can easily cost in the millions.

All of these ideas are valuable and worth looking into. Without further ado, let's get into the real meat of the section: residential real estate investing.

## The Holy Grail: Residential Rental Properties

How do residential rental properties work? Allow me to walk you through a simple example.

You buy a $100,000 single-family rental property (speaking to my midwest peeps for now). Because you get a loan, your initial investment is $30,000, which includes the down payment, closing costs, and make-ready costs. You rent the property for $1,200 per month. Your monthly expenses, including the mortgage payment, insurance, taxes, owner-paid utilities, vacancy, maintenance & repairs, property management, and any other costs, total $870 per month. That means you profit $330 per month. Ta-da! Almost $4,000 per year in passive income.

Investing in rental properties gives you three huge financial benefits:

1) Cash flow or passive income: In the example above, the cash flow is $330 per month, or $3,960 per year, making your cash-on-cash return on investment 13.2%!

2) Equity: not only is your tenant paying your mortgage, essentially giving you a free house over the next thirty years (besides the money you put down), but often real estate appreciates over time. It's not guaranteed, as we saw in 2008, but in thirty years, not only will you own the home free-and-clear without ever making a single mortgage payment, but it could be worth even more by then.

3) Tax benefits: owning a house typically means taking deductions, saving you on money you would otherwise owe the government. Score!

By the way, if you are already discouraged by the above example where the initial investment is $30,000, don't be. In this section, I'm going to teach you everything you need to know about bypassing the typical down payment requirement, whether you're in a low-cost-of-living (LCOL) area or high-cost-of-living (HCOL) city.

*vesting in residential real estate offers three benefits: Cash flow or passive income, equity build up, and tax advantages.*

I'll also show you a couple of strategies that will make this passive income stream accessible for everyone: house hacking and the BRRRR method. By using these, you can get started with way less money. We'll even hear from a couple of people who did this exact thing very successfully.

Now, my dear friends, I could write an entire book—volumes, even—on real estate investing. As of this writing, Andrew and I own five rental properties (35 doors), and the income from those alone is enough to live on should we want to. I also have my realtor's license and understand the ins and outs of making an offer and closing on a property. I'm going to give you as much detail as possible within this chapter, and I've got you covered with some free resources and tools in your *PIAR* Bonus Gift, which can be downloaded at **www.moneyhoneyrachel.com/bonus.** First, a quick detour so we can hear from a real estate mogul himself, David Osborn.

## A Case Study: David Osborn, Multi-Millionaire Real Estate Mogul, Author, & Entrepreneur

David Osborn is unusually impressive. He is one of the most successful real estate franchise owners in the world, has made tens of millions largely due to real estate, and has bought and sold over 1,000 single-family homes. He's also the bestselling author of *Wealth Can't Wait* and co-author of *Miracle Morning Millionaires*. I'm really excited to share his story with you, so you can see exactly how he got started down this notable path. I was super lucky to get to speak with David on the phone and pick his brain.

David has a Mastermind group called "GoBundance," and they have a concept called being a "100-percenter." A 100-percenter is someone who has 100% of their economic needs met by their passive income: If you spend $5,000 per month living, you have $5,000 per month in passive income coming in.

David explained why being a 100-percenter is so cool: *When you're financially free, you can do whatever you want. You can change the world. That's the game. Passive income is not that hard. It's not easy, but it's not like you're designing the next iPhone.*

After graduating from college and working for one year, David went hitchhiking around the world for two years, burning through all his cash. He came back to the US in the mid-1990s with a *negative* net worth of $(1,500) because he had to buy a plane ticket home on his credit card. He was 26 years old. Check out our conversation:

> *When you're financially free, you can do whatever you want. You can change the world. That's the game. Passive income is not that hard. It's not easy, but it's not like you're designing the next iPhone.*
> "
> -David Osborn

Me: *You started down this path at age 26. You were broke and unemployed. What did you do?*

David: *Fortunately, I came home from abroad to my parent's house. My mom was a realtor at that time, and my dad was retired from the military. And my mom said "Hey, look, just come try real estate." I never*

*here have been more*

*millionaires made in*

*real estate than in any*

*other venture in the*

*history of time.*

*thought I'd be a real estate agent because I just didn't think it would be a proper career. But I got into it, I joined my mom, and three years later, we were doing $26 million a year, and we became the #1 team in Keller Williams. So, that's really where I got started digging myself out of my hole, just selling real estate. What I loved about it is that there have been more millionaires made in*

*real estate than in any other venture in the history of time. Real estate creates more wealth than any other business. I can't go design the next Facebook or the next Apple phone, but I can definitely understand how to buy a home, have a payment of $1,000 a month, and rent it out for $1,100 or $1,200 a month. I wanted financial freedom. To me, freedom was very important, and the way I was going to get there was by buying homes.*

David bought his first house in 1995 for $77,000 and put $20,000 down. He still owns it to this day. He lived in it for two years as his residence, and then he moved out and rented it out. In 2001, the value had gone up enough for him to refinance it and take out $60,000 in equity. With that $60,000, he bought three other homes, and those four houses together are worth about $600,000 today. David's net cash flow is $2,800 per month from those four houses. They're all paid for since he put them on 15-year notes. So, from 1995 to 2019, he turned $20K into $600K just on those first four houses.

Me: *You put down $20k for your first house. Was that just from savings you had built up when you were selling homes?*

David: *The great thing about residential sales is that you're not limited. So, my income went up quickly. That money was saved from living at home, no rent, and then just saving that money. I was never an extravagant spender. I got a secondhand car. I never felt the need for the new Gucci loafers. I was not into the new Mercedes. I didn't need any of that stuff.*

David and I talked about learning about positive leverage. Positive leverage is the idea that you borrow money and then make more money than you would have made otherwise. David was very opportunistic in the downtown in 2008-2009. Today, because of leverage, he owns approximately 101 units or doors.

David: *Those 101 units cash-flow about $550,000 a year net. They are all automatic, and I have a great guy that runs it for me, and we have local property managers.*

Me: *At what point did you hire property managers?*

David: *Early on, I tried to do it all myself, and I hated it. And a lot of guys are like, "I'm never going to own property because managing is such a beating." I almost fell into that trap because when someone calls you on a Saturday at four in the morning because the pipe is leaking all over the house, you have to jump up and deal with a flooded house. It'll turn you off really fast when you're only netting $100 a month. Then you're like, "Wait a second, $100 a month, and my life gets ruined?"*

*I was lucky enough to be super into learning and training, and I was around a lot of real estate people. And one of them said, "Why would you not hire a property manager?" He said, "I tip my waiter 15%. All property managers will ask for is 8%." It could have been Robert Kiyosaki who said that. So, I'm probably at about five units at this point, and I followed that advice and hired a property manager. And that was liberating, and then I was like, "Wow, I love this because I don't have to do anything." Just manage the money. And there were ups and downs, there were repairs that happened, but overall, with property managers and a bunch of rentals, you're probably working an hour a month.*

Me: *Do you remember how many hours you worked per week or month when you owned the five rentals but didn't have the property manager yet?*

David: *It would come in spurts. There would be a week that I really didn't have to do anything, and then there would be a couple of repairs one week, and it would be 20 hours. It was never a full-time job.*

Me: *How much was your cash flow on those first five properties?*

David: *The first five were very low. I wanted $100 in free cash flow after all expenses, so I was probably at $500 per month. And remember I had only put $20,000 down, so that's $6,000 a year in cash flow, so that's still a 33% cash-on-cash rate of return. And then there's principal paydown. The cash flow wasn't great, but I was also buying single-family [houses]. I didn't do a lot of multi-family back then.*

Me: *What was one of your biggest mistakes or learning experiences? Did you ever have an "oh $hit" moment?*

David: *The most common mistake is to give a break to your tenant. I had one in particular where the woman just got divorced, and she had two kids and a dog, and I said, "No dogs," and she moved the dog in, and she just kept telling me these sob stories. The next thing you know, a year went by, I'm minus $8,000, I still had to evict her, and she trashed the place on the way out—as if I had done something bad to her. I know her life was tough, and her husband had done something bad and run off with another girl, but—I learned this the hard way—there's no way you mix business with charity.*

> *Assets feed you; liabilities eat you. Never have negative cash flow.*
>
> **"**
>
> -David Osborn

*Another one would be: don't over-leverage. This is a lesson I learned from other people. People would put 90% or 100% leverage on homes. In the two downturns I've seen, I've seen really wealthy people get cleaned out because they over-leveraged their properties, and they put too much debt on it. So, I always try to stay at 80/20 [debt-to-equity ratio] or 70/30. I think when you're starting out, it's okay to go much more leveraged. When you're starting this journey, being much more aggressive is probably smart.*

*Assets feed you; liabilities eat you. Never have negative cash flow. You should have at least $100 per month in pure cash flow, nowadays I try to target $200 per month, and that's after vacancy, after property management, after your mortgage payment. I never buy a negative cash flow.*

Me: *Should everyone invest in real estate? Why or why not?*

David: *Everyone should invest in real estate because it's the everyday man and woman's way to financial freedom. Yes, there are billionaires who strike oil and billionaires that invent new tech, but that's not available to the everyday person. Real estate is available to the everyday person. You need a high school education to be able to add up real estate. You can use sweat to increase the value of the asset. If I buy IBM stock, I can do nothing to affect the value of that stock. But If I buy a house that's a little bit under-repaired, under-looked after, I can put my time in to increase the value of that asset. It requires grit and a little bit of brains.*

*Real estate is a cash-flow-building strategy for the middle class. I know police officers who worked for thirty years on the force and bought ten houses and are financially free because of it.*

> " *Everyone should invest in real estate because it's the everyday man and woman's way to financial freedom.* "
>
> -David Osborn

Me: *The biggest obstacle for a lot of people is that they won't have a ton of money, maybe only a couple of thousand dollars. How can someone with that amount of money get started with real estate investing?*

David: *The first thing is to read a bunch of books. Get educated. And understand that the deal is more important than the money. If you find a really good deal, you can often find a "white knight." I've done this a bunch of times. That's someone who comes along and says, "I'll buy it with you." I know a guy that has built a passive income stream of over $700,000 per year by using investor money, and he's always paid them between 8% and 10%. Because he had such faith and did such due diligence, he found good deals. He would go to people and say, "Look, I need 20% down. Loan me $20,000, and I'll pay you $2,000 per year, and I have the right to pay you off at any time." So, that's one way to do it, that's a more aggressive way. The best way for a person to get into real estate is to buy a house for themselves, with the intention, always, of turning it into a rental within 12-24 months.*

David concludes with the following: *Financial freedom is available for everyone. If I'm a C-student, barely made it through college in 5.5 years, and barely ever made the honor roll, and I can become financially free through real estate, then anyone can. And I'm here to help. When you reach a certain level of success, the greatest achievement is pouring into others and figuring out how to help them get their dreams fulfilled, and that's really what leaves a legacy. That's what I'm all about.*

Wow! I have chills! You can learn more about David's journey and contact him through his website, www.DavidOsborn.com. Also, make sure to read his two books, *Wealth Can't Wait* and *Miracle Morning Millionaires*. You can follow David on social media as well.

Facebook: www.facebook.com/DavidOsbornWCW

Instagram: www.instagram.com/iamdavidosborn

Twitter: www.twitter.com/IAmDavidOsborn

We're about to jump into all the creative ways you can fund your first rental property. You will learn the ins and outs of house hacking and the BRRRR method, hear from a couple of people who successfully used these strategies, and also learn how to invest if you're in a HCOL area.

# CHAPTER 20:

# *First, Funding...*

The most common question I get regarding how to get into real estate investing is, "How can I start without a ton of money?" This chapter will address precisely that. We'll weigh the benefits of cash vs. leveraging and then get into some specific strategies to avoid large down payment requirements: namely, house hacking and the BRRRR method. I'll also talk about what people in a HCOL area can do.

## Cash vs. Leveraging

Some investors feel strongly about buying a property with cash, and others feel strongly about leveraging their money using a mortgage. I'll talk about the pros and cons of both.

To buy a property with cash, you need money. We're talking if a property is listed for $330,000, you're buying it with $330,000 of liquid cash. No loans involved. The distinct disadvantage is that this takes even more capital since you're buying it outright instead of coming up with a down payment on a loan.

With a mortgage, you're leveraging your money. Leveraging means you're using borrowed money to generate an even higher profit; you put some money down and borrow the rest to lower your initial investment. The trouble is, with leverage comes risk, and it got a lot of people in trouble in 2008. Let's say you put $10K down on a $100K property, so you have an $90K loan. Then the housing bubble bursts, prices fall, and suddenly your property is worth $80K. But your loan is still $90K. That means you are underwater on your mortgage: you owe more than it's worth. You never want to be in that position! That's one reason why, after 2008, lenders became stricter with their requirements (although there's mixed feedback on whether they *really* tightened things up.) The bottom line is that leveraging your money is riskier than buying it outright.

> " Leveraging means you're using borrowed money to generate an even higher profit... with

When you buy with cash, you have no mortgage payment, which eliminates the largest "expense." I put that in quotes because, often, when an investor is evaluating their rental income, they don't count their mortgage as a strict expense since part of that mortgage payment goes towards principal pay-down, thereby building equity in the home. Many investors hone in on Net Operating Income (NOI), which is your revenue minus all of your expenses except for the mortgage payment. When I talk about rental properties, though, I want to know the bottom-line monthly cash flow, *after* the mortgage payment has been made. When you leverage, you normally have a twenty-, twenty-five-, or thirty-year mortgage on which you have to make payments every month, eating into your cash flow.

I'm a firm believer in leveraging your money. I feel very safe and secure, especially when I'm required to put 25% down as an investor. I plan to hold onto these for the long term, which means if prices go down, I should be able to withstand the market until they go back up, instead of selling and taking a loss. I play the long game. Plus, I wouldn't be where I am today if I had bought properties with all cash. In fact, I probably wouldn't own a single property. Most twenty-somethings don't have a cool $100,000 lying around to invest. Leveraging makes it possible for more people to own real estate.

For investment properties, lenders typically require you to put 20% to 25% down on the property, but don't write off this passive income idea just because you don't have $20,000. House hacking and the BRRRR method will help you bypass this requirement.

## House Hacking

Let us behold the beauty of h hacking. House hacking is v you buy a multifamily prop such as a duplex or a triplex quad. You live in one unit as primary residence, and you out the other unit(s) to offset mortgage and potentially gen positive cash flow on top of th

*House Hacking and the BRRRR method make it easier for anyone to invest in real estate without having a ton of money.*

Why is this so cool? Since you intend to use the property as your primary residence, you are an owner-occupant. Owner-occupants get the lowest interest rates and the lowest down payment requirements. If you live in the property, down payments as low as 0% to 5% are possible with programs like VA and FHA loans. If you don't qualify for those, you could qualify for conventional loans with only 5%, 10%, or 15% down and then pay private mortgage insurance (PMI). That means *you don't need a ton of money to do this.*

For example, a husband and wife buy a $200,000 triplex (totally realistic for some markets. Our first duplex in Louisville, KY cost $100,000 in 2017. Patience, HCOL grasshoppers.) Because the husband and wife are first-time homebuyers and qualify for an FHA loan, they only need to put down 3.5%, or $7,000.

Now, remember, we just talked about how high leverage means high risk. The less you put down on a property, the riskier it could be in a volatile market. The last thing you want to do is end up underwater on your mortgage, so make sure you fully understand the risks here.

When making an offer on the $200K triplex, the husband and wife negotiate for the seller to pay closing costs and prepaids. The triplex could use some updates but is move-in ready. Let's say that their grand total initial investment, including the inspection, appraisal, and some other miscellaneous fees, is $8,700.

Two of the three units are already renting for $1,000 each, or $2,000 total. The husband and wife move into the third unit.

Here's the kicker, though: The $2,000 per month in rental income not only covers all the expenses, it also generates $50/month in positive cash flow!

Over the next two years, the husband and wife can do one of two things:

1) Live for free in their triplex and save aggressively. They save the money that they otherwise would have spent on rent or a mortgage payment. After two years, they have $19,000 in savings. They then use that to buy another rental property, which would increase their rental income even more.

2) Use the money they are saving in living expenses plus the extra $50/month to begin fixing up the property and increasing their equity. They upgrade a few of the older appliances in the other units. They repaint and re-carpet some of the worn-down areas. They renovate two of the older bathrooms and fill in the potholes in the driveway and parking spots. All in all, over the next two years, they take the money that they would have spent on their own rent or mortgage and invest another $19,000 into upgrading the property. The triplex that they bought for $200,000 is now worth $250,000 because of the upgrades!

House hacking can be done in a multitude of ways. In the above example, the husband and wife used house hacking to buy a rental property without a large down payment. Others may conduct a live-in flip. A live-in flip is where you buy a single-family house that needs a lot of work, fix it up while living there for two years, and sell it for a profit. Because you are the owner-occupant in this scenario as well, you do not need a large down payment.

Why do I keep suggesting two years? First, most mortgage companies require that you live in the property as your primary residence for at least 12 months, but sometimes up to 24 months, so you must understand all the requirements. If you attempt to move out of the property before the required amount of time, you could be on the line for mortgage fraud.

Another component of the two-year rule has to do with capital gains taxes. Sometimes when you sell a house for more than you bought it, you'll have to pay a capital gains tax. In other words, if you buy a $200K triplex and then sell it immediately for $250K, you'll likely have to pay capital gains taxes. To avoid paying capital gains taxes, you must live in the house for two out of the last five years. And there's a max on this rule—your profit can't exceed $250,000 as a single owner or $500,000 as a married owner. Another way to avoid capital gains taxes is by doing a 1031 exchange, which is something you can research and discuss with your CPA.

## The BRRRR Method

Either in concurrence with house hacking or utilized on its own is another technique that makes it easy to continue buying rentals after the first one. This is where someone buys, renovates, and rents a property, and then refinances it in order to pull out equity. That equity is then used to purchase the next property. This method is widely known as the BRRRR method: Buy, Rehab, Rent, Refinance, Repeat. The BRRRR method is a term coined and created by *BiggerPockets*.

Jen Reeves, the owner of Exceptional Homes based out of Ohio, is a perfect example of the BRRRR method done successfully.

Jen and her husband started by house hacking with a live-in flip on their first, primary residence. Their home needed cosmetic updates, which Jen and her husband completed over two years. The upgrades cost around $12,000. They sold the house after two years for an $18,000 profit, and they used that capital to buy their next property.

Their next property was a for-sale-by-owner property that had been horribly maintained, so it needed quite a bit of rehab. Jen explains, "The renovation took us about three months, which we mostly DIY'd, and the bulk of that labor was spent on cigarette smoke remediation."

Here comes the BRRRR method. After one year, the house appraised for $155,000, which was about twice as much as they bought it for, and they were able to take out a home equity line for $57,000. They rented the house out and had a huge chunk of money to invest in the next property.

Today, they own five single-family rentals. Their goal is to net $3,000 per month, and they believe they can do that within the next year. The $3,000 per month goal is deliberate, "as that amount would technically cover all of our monthly expenses should we desire (or need) to step away from our current jobs." It even covers health insurance! Jen and her husband live in a fairly low-cost-of-living area in Ohio. Once the mortgages are paid off, she estimates that they'll be profiting $7,000 per month, which will provide plenty of buffer.

So how passive was this process for them, really? To save on money in the beginning, Jen and her husband did most of the work themselves, so it was time-intensive. But as they've repeated the BRRRR process, they've hired out more of the work. Their latest rehab was much more hands-off. The BRRRR method is one that takes more time but costs less money. This method proves that anyone can get started with rental property investing even if they don't have a ton of capital. Jen estimates that on a month with no turnovers, she spends less than two hours on bookkeeping and maintenance requests. "It's far more passive than any job that would earn us the same amount per month!"

> *investing] is far more passive than any job that would earn us the same amount per month!*
>
> -Jen Reeves

Jen says, *"Due to the effectiveness of BRRRR over the past three and a half years, we have just about tripled our initial capital, factoring in the equity we have accumulated. For someone starting out, I think completing live-in flips are a great way to build capital. If you can live in the home for at least two years, you can sell it and walk away, potentially with a completely tax-free profit."*

That's the BRRRR method in a nutshell. House hacking makes it easy to buy your first property, and then following BRRRR—Buy, Rehab, Rent, Refinance, Repeat—makes it easy to buy your second, third, fourth, and tenth property. But even with these strategies, it can be tough for those in a HCOL area to get into real estate investing. Up next, we'll discuss one strategy to consider in this circumstance.

## What if I live in a HCOL area?

Some of you may live in New York City, Denver, Nashville, Los Angeles, San Diego... or really anywhere in California where housing costs are exorbitant. I won't be subtle about it: it's a lot harder to find good deals in these areas where properties already cost so much. A 25% down payment on a $700,000 duplex would be $175,000. I can count on one hand the number of people I know personally that have that kind of money sitting in the bank.

Besides house hacking and the BRRRR method, which are both viable solutions for HCOL areas, I encourage you to also consider long-distance landlording. For example, do you have family in another town? Do you have connections in the mid-west? Did you move to NYC from Ohio? Did you move to LA from St. Louis? Are there any other cities you are familiar with or where you have family or a network of contacts? Those are the cities to consider for long-distance landlording. Or, are there cheaper properties that are an hour or two away from where you live that you can still handle by yourself? Lots to think about!

Can you begin working with a realtor in another city and set up a property search? Do you know anyone there who can check out the properties you are interested in? If not, when's the next time you're going home to visit? I'm not saying that finding a property in another city will be easy, but if you want to make this passive income stuff happen, you'll find a way.

Managing tenants from far away sounds daunting, I know, but it's a good alternative. I have a friend that used to live in Hawaii and, instead of selling when she moved, she kept the house and rented it out. She manages it well enough from an entire ocean away! She had a long-term tenant for three years; when that tenant gave notice, she considered flying back for a week to A) visit and vaca, and B) get it re-rented, but in the end, she didn't need to. She re-rented it quickly and with ease from afar.

Here's what she had to say: *I have not yet experienced a single day of vacancy on the property, and I have never even shown the property. In order to do all of this remotely, I need three things: adequate time to find and qualify the right tenant, a compelling value proposition, and digital marketing tools.*

*Overall, real estate investment is all about strategy. The numbers have to work, either through cash flow or through great appreciation of your asset. Sometimes neither of these things can be found where you are living. In this case, the only option is to search for a property that is not local to you. Of course, it is ideal to have your properties nearby, but I am proof that it's possible to manage assets from half a world away! I'd encourage anyone to broaden their scope and shop outside of their geographical area. If you can establish a couple of good relationships where your properties are, and if you can make phone calls, you can do everything a property management company would do!*

As a long-distance landlord, you can rely on family or friends, or you can pay someone to show and lease your properties for you. A realtor is the best person to hire, given his or her experience and professionalism, but you could also find another landlord in the area, a property management company, or someone else.

In fact, David Greene, co-host of the wildly successful podcast *BiggerPockets,* is a long-distance landlord. By day, he's a police officer in San Francisco; by night, he's one of the most successful self-made real estate investors around—and it all started when he purchased rental properties out-of-state. He popularized the term BRRRR, and he now owns dozens of rental properties using this method. For more information, I highly recommend checking out his podcast *BiggerPockets* or nabbing one of his books—they're all fantastic!

Now, if you're *still* not satisfied with this proposal, don't worry. We're about to hear from another real estate entrepreneur, Doug Skipworth. He has even more unique ideas for getting into real estate investing without having tons of cash.

## A Case Study: Doug Skipworth, Real Estate Mogul & Co-Founder of Crestcore Realty

For all that he has achieved in his 18 years of real estate, Doug Skipworth is incredibly down-to-earth and humble. Not only is Doug a CPA and CFA, but he also co-founded Crestcore Realty in 2001 and has helped real estate investors purchase over 1,000 properties. Crestcore now manages over 2,500 residential properties in Memphis, TN, and Doug personally owns hundreds of those properties himself. I spoke with Doug on the phone to pick his brain on all things real estate investing.

Me: *Why did you want to get started investing in the first place?*

Doug: *Real estate is a means to an end. Passive rental income fit into what I was looking to do for my own business and personal growth, so I saw that as a piece of the puzzle.*

Doug started investing in 2007 when he was 33 years old. (He admitted that one of his two regrets is that he didn't start younger.) His first investment was a $45,000 single-family rental property in Tennessee. He had some equity in his residence, so he borrowed against that equity to buy the property outright. Doug started out by explaining how he used the BRRRR method:

Doug: *When I was 33, I didn't have a lot of cash sitting around. I had equity in my home, but I didn't have $45,000 sitting in the bank where I could buy something. The first rental property cost $45,000 in cash for the purchase price. Then I had to put another $5,000 in for renovation and repair work. That was in Memphis, TN. So, I had $50,000 in that first property, all of which was borrowed out of my home equity line. So, I had borrowed $50,000 and then I went to the bank and got an appraisal, and the house appraised for $70,000. Then, I got a mortgage for $50,000 and repaid myself, so I could then go and do #2. That's the BRRRR method. So, it was kind of a rinse and repeat.*

Doug repeated the BRRRR process about six times on his own before connecting with Dan Butler, his current business partner. He met Dan when they lived in the same neighborhood and started jogging together. They shared some common real estate interests and finally decided to do a deal together.

Me: *When and why did you decide to partner up with Dan?*

Doug: *We did a small experiment. I heard this example the other day: "If you want to learn and you have $1,000, go to the $1 table and play a thousand hands to figure it out, don't go to the $1,000 table and play once." Dan and I are the same way. We had each bought houses several times, but we had never bought through a tax sale. So, we thought, "Hey, why don't we share the risk on this and just try one together?" So, we tried one together; it was only $12,000, so $6,000 apiece.*

Me: *What is your advice for people who are husbands or wives or who want to do this with a partner?*

Doug: *I totally recommend partners. It's been the best business decision I've made. I would say you need to align the vision, so making sure the partners are all on the same page with the big "why." I've always viewed Dan as the senior partner and me as the junior, and he does the same thing. It's kind of like a marriage or any type of long-term relationship—you have to serve the other if you're going to make this for the long term. It can't be all about you.*

Me: *When you were starting out, were you managing everything yourself?*

Doug: *I did choose to self-manage. And that took a little more time, but I had more time than I did money. So, I was willing to give up some mornings, nights, weekends, to save a dollar, where other people might choose to pay a manager. Either way, you're paying—you're paying with your time or with your money. So, when I was 33, I was paying with time. I wanted to learn, get my feet wet, and figure out what I was doing before I hired a manager.*

Me: *When you had your first or second property, how many hours per week were you spending to manage your property?*

Doug: *On average, I would say an hour per week. That might be three hours one week and zero hours for a couple of weeks. However, I was probably putting at least three to five hours per week into researching the next deal, learning all I could, attending classes, networking, things like that. So, I was working "on" the business, even though I was really working in the business for one hour.*

Me: *At what point did you start hiring property managers?*

Doug: *We probably had 250 units before we hired them.*

Me: *Oh my gosh! You were managing 250 rentals on your own?!*

Doug: *Yes. *Laughs.* Dan and I together, you know. We were both working full-time. I had some flexibility with my business.*

> **would call [rental income] passive. I would call it Mailbox Money.**
>
> -Doug Skipworth

Doug explains to me that he was working 40-hour weeks just on his rental property business—in addition to a full-time job! He and Dan were seriously putting in the time.

Me: *My mind is blown. Wow! So now you have employees, and you're not directly managing them anymore. In terms of real estate investing, do you think it's truly passive, or can it be truly passive?*

Doug: *There's always—besides maybe annuities, royalties—there is some aspect of "manage the manager," but I would call it passive. I would call it Mailbox Money. Absolutely, it is possible to do that.*

Me: *I think real estate investing is such an important wealth-building tool. I believe everyone should own a rental property. What do you think?*

Doug: *Absolutely, I agree. We have 750 clients who we manage property for, and they are doing it for all types of reasons. Some are doing it for wealth creation, some are doing it for cash flow, some are doing it for financial freedom, but most everybody has a goal. To me, real estate is a great tool to assist people in realizing their dreams. We always tell people, "Don't wait to buy real estate. Buy real estate and wait." That's the mantra we preach.*

> 'on't wait to buy real estate. Buy real estate and wait. "
>
> -Doug Skipworth

Me: *If someone doesn't have a lot of money or equity in a house like you did, if someone only has a few thousand dollars, how can they get started in real estate investing?*

Doug has tons of exciting suggestions for this, so to make it easier, I'll put them in a list form:

- REITs: *There's always real estate investing through the stock market via REITs.*

- Roofstock[40]: *Some people are trying to bridge that gap between full-fledged property ownership and then the faceless, nameless, REIT. There're some hybrids out there: Roofstock is an example where they're selling a fractional interest in rental houses, so that is another little small step. Roofstock is in its infancy, but they see a need; there's a hole in the market, and they're trying to fill it.*

- Partner up: *Find a partner, and maybe the partner has some equity or financial resource, and maybe you can put in more sweat while they put in more money. Maybe you have something to bring to the table that they don't.*

- Fannie Mae Investor Loans[41]: *Fannie Mae has their investor loan program. That's my second regret. My first regret is that I didn't start before age 33, and my second regret is that I didn't use Fannie Mae investor loans initially to buy and build a 10-house portfolio that's appreciating and cash-flowing on a 30-year amortization. That is a great program that we've seen a lot.*

- Go to a community bank: *If you develop a plan and you go to community banks, a community bank will listen to your story. If you have a really good story, they might get behind you and fund you and give you a line of credit called a guidance line.*

- Owner-Financing: *One thing we've done a whole bunch of is owner-financing. A great way for people to get into real estate investing is by approaching an owner who is in a position to carry a mortgage. So, the owner finances the property. We've done many a deal where we haven't had to put any money down, and sometimes they'll finance it at 0% interest. Maybe you pay more for the property than someone else would, or maybe there's some other reason they'd want to work with you. Owner financing has been a tool we've used a ton.*

Me: *What else would you like my readers to know about you and your business?*

Doug: *I love to set goals, and I love to connect people. I am happy to help any and everybody I can. In high school, I played basketball, I was a point guard, and I loved nothing more than to get the ball to other people on the team. We have a great team, so if we ever need to help anybody buying property, managing property, or lending on property, we can do all those things. I'm happy to connect people to that and to all the resources we have. We'd love to hear from anybody.*

You can check out Doug's website at www.CrestCore.com to get in touch with him and his team. Make sure to follow him on social media.

Facebook: www.facebook.com/crestcorerealtyllc

Instagram: www.instagram.com/crestcorerealty

Twitter: www.twitter.com/CrestCore

There you have it: how to fund your rental properties. If you can't swing the normal 20% to 25% down payment requirement, we've discussed a plethora of ideas in this chapter: house hacking, live-in flips, the BRRRR method, and long-distance landlording. Both David and Doug gave us even more suggestions that are great for those with less capital. Now that you know how to fund your real estate property, it's time to learn how to *find* your real estate property.

# CHAPTER 21

## ...Followed by Finding

You've learned the ins and outs of funding your first rental property, which is the biggest obstacle for people who want to get their foot in the door. Now it's time to learn how to find your first rental property.

### Looking for Properties

The very first step is to think about what kind of property you want to invest in. Here are four parameters to consider:

1) Location: Location is the most crucial factor. You'll want to consider crime rates, which areas are up-and-coming, and how far you're willing to drive. All of my rentals are within a 30-minute drive, and I personally wouldn't want to go farther than that, but I'm also a little spoiled in Louisville, KY. Your goal is to narrow down the specific areas on a map where you would be open to investing.

2) Property type: The main property types to consider are single-family, duplex, triplex, or quad. As a beginner, you'll want to stay within four units or less because often you need to get a commercial loan for anything over four units, and also, we want to walk before we run. The advantage of multiple units is that even if one unit is vacant, the others are still paying rent, and that helps maintain your cash flow. Another advantage is that the multi-family market tends to be less volatile than single-family.

3) Price: In some cases, you'll have to put 20% to 25% down on a rental property. Lenders tend to impose stricter requirements on properties that are bought as investments rather than as primary residences. Think about what would be a realistic goal for you if you're going this route. If you don't have a hefty down payment saved up, you can consider using one of the strategies we discussed in Chapter 20.

4) Condition. Do you want to buy something that's already rented and in good shape, or do you want to buy something you'll need to renovate and then rent? (Do you have the money for the latter?)

You'll also need to build a team. At the very least, you should find a trustworthy realtor, lender, and insurance agent. These guys will help you from the very beginning before you even put an offer in, so make sure you select who you want to work with now.

In terms of finding the property, you can try several things. The most obvious way is working with a realtor to look at listings on the Multiple Listing Service (MLS). A realtor will have the timeliest information and will coordinate the entire transaction for you. Also, as a buyer, you do not pay the realtor's commission. Real estate commissions are a widely misunderstood concept. In a typical deal, the seller pays the commission for both the buyer's agent and the seller's agent. You pay nothing to work with a realtor as a buyer.

Working with a realtor on the MLS isn't the only way to buy real estate. In fact, it can be challenging to find deals this way because everyone does it; it's the most accessible and, therefore, the most competitive. If you want to find deals faster, you'll need to get creative. Here are a few other ways to find deals on properties that aren't necessarily listed for sale on the market.

## Short Sales & Pre-Foreclosures

A short sale may happen when someone is underwater on their home, meaning they owe more on the mortgage than the home is worth. In this case, the lender may agree to accept a mortgage payoff amount less than what is owed to facilitate a sale of the property by a financially distressed owner; it's the bank's way of accepting a small loss to avoid an even greater one. That's called a short sale. Often, people in pre-foreclosure may qualify for a short sale. It may damage their credit, but a foreclosure would be worse. The buyer gets the property at a reduced price.

Owners of distressed properties who are having financial difficulties might not know that a short sale is a potential option. If you can find these owners, you can speak with them about facilitating a short sale in which you are the buyer. Once you get the lender to agree, it's a good way to buy at a reduced price. Unfortunately, some unethical people take advantage of homeowners by talking them into this when it may not be their best option, so some view this practice as shady. But if it's truly the right route for all involved, it can be a good thing.

You can buy lists or contact attorneys or mortgage companies to find homeowners who are late on their mortgage payments or who are in pre-foreclosure. From there, it's a matter of reaching out and having a conversation with the homeowner, then working with a professional who can facilitate the short sale.

## Auctions

When it's too late for a homeowner to do a short sale, their house may be put up for auction in a foreclosure sale. Homes may also be sold at auctions if the owner doesn't pay property taxes. Buying at auction is riskier and doesn't allow for an inspection. Often, you must have all cash, meaning you must front the capital or work with a private money lender.

You can find foreclosure auctions or tax deed auctions by contacting your local government, local sheriff, or county clerk.

## REO

When a bank fails to sell a foreclosure at auction, then they typically take ownership, and it becomes a Real Estate Owned (REO) property. The lender will then try to sell it themselves. If you can find these leads right away through a bank contact or an agent that works REO deals, you can put in an offer before the bank lists it on the MLS. At this point, banks usually are desperate to sell, and you can get a good deal.

## Probate

When a homeowner passes away, the property either is passed on to whomever the owner specified in the will, or the property is passed on to the probate court to be sold. To find a probate lead, you'll usually need to go to the courthouse and get a list, or you can buy a list from someone who does this. You can contact the person in the will (often, a family member of the deceased person), but this can be hurtful to the family, as they may be in emotional distress. On the other hand, many people in probate live out of state or are stressed at the idea of having to care for a property and want to get rid of the property quickly, and that's where you can potentially help. If you are sensitive and ethical, it can absolutely be a way for everyone to win.

## "Driving for Dollars"

Driving for dollars is a fun phrase for driving or walking around a neighborhood looking for vacant or distressed properties. You can leave flyers at the property or write down the addresses and look up the owner so that you can get in touch with him or her directly. You may also happen upon an out-of-state landlord that is having trouble maintaining the property and who may be motivated to sell.

## Bandit Signs

Bandit signs are those signs you see around your community that say "We Buy Houses" with a phone number. First and foremost, check your city ordinances to find out if and where you can place these signs. If you're in the clear, they can be very effective for generating leads (even though they may seem tacky). You can put these up in your target area and wait for calls to roll in from motivated sellers.

## Networking

Never underestimate the power of networking. The more people you know, the better chance you have of someone sending you a good lead or thinking of you when they come upon a distressed property. You should connect with attorneys, property management companies, landlords, and investors. You can even join an investor association in your city to begin meeting people. Associations are a great way to connect with wholesalers, who find great deals and get them under contract, and then are paid a fee by people like you that want to take over the contract and close on the property. Wholesaling is another great way to get into real estate investing with zero money. You find the deal and wholesale it to another investor who will pay you a few thousand dollars for doing the legwork.

## Call FSBO

You can also look at For Sale By Owner listings and websites and reach out to those sellers. If you can offer them a quick sale or if they are motivated, they may agree to a lower price.

## Expired Listings

I found my first duplex by searching the expired and canceled listings on the MLS and reaching out to the listing agent. It turned out to be one of the best deals I've ever done. The listing had expired and had been sitting for a while, and I got in touch with the sellers right before they re-listed. You can work with a realtor to come up with a list of expired or canceled listings.

## Analyzing the Property

Let's say you've done all your homework so far. You've defined some parameters in terms of location, property type, price, and condition. You have a realtor, lender, and insurance agent ready to go, and you've started the property search.

What do you do when you find a potential property? *Run the numbers.*

Even before I look at a property in person, I run the numbers. I don't want to waste my time on something that won't make a good investment in the first place.

*For some quick, high-level insight, use the 1% rule.*

What does running the numbers look like? You'll start with revenues, subtract expenses, and do some math and fancy equations to come to a conclusion.

For some quick, initial, high-level insight, I use the 1% rule. The 1% rule says that for every $100,000 of price, the property should generate $1,000 per month in rental income. Take heed: the 1% rule is a *general* guideline, not a metric by which to make your decision.

The 1% rule helps me because if I see a property that's listed for $275,000, but it only gets $1,800 per month in rent, I know right away that's not a good deal. It's listed way too high. Do I write it off right then? Maybe, maybe not. There's always a chance that someone will come off their list price, and that you can buy it for significantly less than $275,000. But according to the 1% rule, the list price should be closer to $180,000, and I don't think it's likely to negotiate down that far. I use the 1% rule as a quick guideline to tell me which properties are worth investigating further.

If something has potential based on the 1% rule, then you'll *really* run the numbers.

You'll start with what you believe you can rent the property for. If the property is currently rented, you'll use the current rent. You can definitely make a note of any potential upside if you think it's under-rented, but *actual* rents are far more reliable than *potential* rents. If the property is not rented, you can do some research using Zillow, Craigslist, or other sites to find similar properties listed for rent. This will again give you an estimate— not a certainty—of what the property could rent for per month. Be conservative!

Then you'll estimate all of your monthly expenses. These will include:

- Mortgage payment (your lender will help you estimate this, or you can use an online calculator)
- Property taxes (you can look up tax records to see what the current owner pays and come up with an estimate)
- Insurance (your insurance agent will help you estimate this)
- Utilities, if paid by owner (a realtor can help you get this information)
  - Water
  - Sewer
  - Gas
  - Electric
  - Trash

- Homeowners Association fee or condo fee
- Landscaping or snow removal
- Pest control
- Maintenance and repair
- Capital investment (a portion of money set aside each month for the larger investments over time like a new roof or HVAC)
- Vacancy (your property won't be rented 100% of the time so you must account for the gaps between tenants; a reasonable estimate is 8%)
- Property management
- Miscellaneous (catch-all for anything you forgot)

Not all of these expenses would necessarily apply to you, but they are items worth considering. Keep in mind these should all be monthly expense estimates. You want to be conservative on all these numbers. You are literally going to make your decision based on this, so give yourself a buffer. And then *more* buffer. The last thing you want is to buy the property and realize you miscalculated something *in the wrong direction*. I've had that happen once... not fun. What you should hope for is to be so conservative with your estimates that your property does better than what you projected.

Total up the expenses. Subtract the expenses from the rent revenue. What's left? Your estimated cash flow.

## Metrics

Before going any further, you need to understand these three metrics to determine whether a property makes a good investment. They are:

1) Monthly cash flow
2) Cash on cash ROI
3) Capitalization rate

Your cash flow is your profit; it's what's left after expenses are paid. It's your rent minus all of your costs (including the mortgage payment.) Everyone has different cash flow requirements. What's *not* an acceptable cash flow is zero or a negative number. Why? Because our goal with this book is to generate passive income. Sure, a zero-cash-flow property could still be a good investment from a long-term, equity perspective, but we are trying to create income, not just buy an appreciating asset. We are looking for positive cash flow.

When I first began looking, I wanted something that would generate at least $200 to $300 per month. The first actual property I bought produced more like $500. And now, as I've grown my portfolio, my requirements have increased. What was right for me may not necessarily be right for you. Ask yourself what monthly profit would make it worth it to you. If you need $4,000 per month to retire, and you want at least $100 per month per property in cash flow, then you'll need to acquire forty properties. If you want $800 per month per property in cash flow, you'll need to acquire five properties. Oh, and just because you say you want $2,000 per month in cash flow from one property doesn't mean that's realistic. Depending on your market, you may need to lower your minimum.

Your <u>cash on cash ROI</u> shows you how much bang you're getting for each buck you invest. Here's how it's calculated:

*Cash on cash ROI = (Annual cash flow) / (Total initial investment)*

Annual cash flow is simply your monthly cash flow times 12. Your total initial investment will consist of your down payment, inspection, appraisal, closing costs, renovations, and any other money you put into the property to get it ready to rent. When you're leveraging your money and using a mortgage, you're only actually fronting the down payment. When you're buying it outright, then your initial investment will be the entire purchase price. You can see how it's easier to get a higher ROI with leverage.

As an example, let's say you buy a $160,000 duplex. You put 25% down, which is $40,000, and have another $5,000 in other costs, so your total initial investment is $45,000.

Let's say that your cash flow analysis projects $400 per month in profit, which is $4,800 per year.

That makes your cash on cash ROI = 4,800 / 45,000 = 10.7%.

Is that good or bad? I could give you my subjective opinion, but only YOU can be the judge of what constitutes a good enough ROI for you. When I first started out, I figured, "Well, I want to earn at least more than what I could make in the stock market, because if not, why wouldn't I just invest in the stock market?"

The stock market's average return over the long run is around 10%, depending on how you look at it and who you ask. Therefore, I wanted at least an 11% or 12% return on my rental property.

But you might disagree. You might hate the stock market and not trust it or not want to compare it to a long-term average, and that's fair. Maybe you want at least an 8% ROI. Or maybe 12% still isn't worth it to you, and you want 14%. Go for it! You make the rules here.

Finally, you'll want to take a look at your <u>capitalization rate</u>. Put simply, the cap rate calculates what the ROI would be if you bought the property outright. Your cap rate shows you what the asset itself is generating as a return. Here is the calculation:

*Capitalization rate = (Annual cash flow) / (Property value)*

Most often, for property value, you'll estimate the price at which you'll buy the property. Let's use the above example with the $160,000 duplex:

Cap rate = 4,800 / 160,000 = 3%

As with the other metrics, I can't tell you what a good or bad rate is. 3% feels low, but cap rates are not something I rely on, and in some cases, I don't even calculate it. The bottom line for me comes down to cash flow and cash on cash ROI. A cap rate can be used as a good comparative tool to see what other properties in the area are yielding and whether yours is better or worse. Use it more directionally than anything else. It's an important metric that helps you evaluate your risk, and it's worth understanding. Lower cap rate = lower return. Higher cap rate = higher return.

As I mentioned before, some investors prefer to look at NOI instead of cash flow. NOI takes your revenue minus all your expenses except for the mortgage payment. You are getting some benefit from the mortgage payment since you're building equity in a home, so it makes sense to remember this isn't a true "expense" like some of the other items. However, our goal is to have positive cash flow, not just positive NOI; we want actual, profitable cash flow every month because that what is it means to have passive income. Passive income = financial independence, and that's the goal.

## Making an offer

If you've found a property that meets all your requirements, it's time to make an offer. Scary, I know! But also exciting.

When you make an offer, it helps if you have a preapproval letter and/or proof of funds. These make your offer look stronger to the seller.

Making an offer is not just about the purchase price. You'll want to consider several other aspects. A realtor will help you with them.

- Are you going to ask for the appliances to remain with the property?

- Are you going to ask for an inspection? Hint: Yes.

- Are you going to ask the seller to pay for your closing costs?

- Do you want to close with a specific company?

- Do you want a home warranty?

- How much time do you need before you close?

- How much earnest money will you be offering?

The less you ask for, the more competitive your offer. But some of those things might be a deal maker or breaker for you, so it's important to think them all through.

Once you send in the offer, the seller may accept, counter, or reject. You may go through a couple of rounds of negotiations. But once you have an accepted contract, the next step is home inspections. After that, depending on your contract, you'll have an opportunity to ask for or negotiate repairs to be completed by the seller before closing. Then, you'll apply for the loan and order the appraisal, which your lender helps you with. Finally, you'll close on the property and officially be the owner of a rental!

Which begs the question: what now? Keep reading to find out how to find good tenants and a property manager.

# CHAPTER 22

# *Avoiding Tenant Nightmares*

Make no mistake: investing in real estate comes with its fair share of nightmares. Talk to any landlord, and you'll find that most agree that dealing with tenants is one of the most frustrating aspects of owning rental property. In this chapter, we'll talk about how to find good tenants, which will help you avoid and prevent many of the major tenant issues and hassles, and how to hire a property manager so that you don't have to deal with tenants at all.

## Tenants

At last... you can start collecting rent. At this point, you're in one of three situations:

1) You inherited tenants

2) You bought a vacant property and need to find tenants

3) A mix of both if it's multi-unit

When you inherit tenants, you can't do much until their lease expires. Leases do not go away when a property is bought and sold.

Let me repeat that: A lease is a lease. It does not get canceled when property ownership changes hands.

Now, if the tenant is breaking the lease, that's a different story. But you can't expect to buy a property and start raising the rent or kicking tenants out when they still have three months to go on their lease.

If you inherited good tenants in a good situation, you might not want to do much except continue operations. You'll want to introduce yourself via a letter and in person and reassure them that nothing will change for the remainder of their lease. You'll want to check in with them every so often and ensure they are taking care of the place. You'll want to pick up rent each month.

Ah, that's the good life.

More often than not, you'll need to find new tenants. Either you're waiting out your current tenant's lease so that you can replace that tenant, or you need to rent out a property you bought that's currently vacant.

Finding good tenants is the most essential part of the business. They will make or break you. Allow me to repeat that. Your tenants will make or break you. Ensure that you are screening them *as much as possible* before entrusting them with your property.

The best way to find tenants is to advertise online: Zillow, Trulia, and even Craigslist. Many websites make it easy for you to post to multiple sites at once. I use Cozy, which is a platform for managing rentals. Not only can you advertise on it, but you can also review tenant applications and set up a direct deposit for rent collection.

Another great way to find tenants is to put a For Rent sign out front. Back when I worked in my first real estate investment job, I nearly rolled my eyes when it was suggested that I go put up a sign to generate leads. Alas, I was proven wrong. We got more calls from that sign than anything else. Not having one is an enormous mistake.

Think of some pre-screen questions to help you weed out some of the people who might not be a good fit for your unit. (By the way, legally, you have to show the property to anyone and everyone who wants to see it, unless you're exempt from the federal Fair Housing Act.) Do you accept pets? If not, it might be something to ask them. Smoking or nonsmoking?

And for goodness sake, don't discriminate. If you are unsure if something is discrimination, consult with a realtor or attorney.

From there, you'll do showings with potential tenants. It goes without saying to make sure the property looks and smells as good as possible before you show it. To look even more professional, come to the showing with flyers for the property and application instructions.

You can make your own application and manually order credit and background checks, but I find it much easier to use an online platform that will do everything for you. Typically, the applicant will be required to pay a fee to cover the cost of the credit and background check, and that fee will either go to you if you are doing it or to the platform you are using.

You'll screen applications by calling through their past landlord references, calling for employment verification, and ensuring everything else checks out. You can also require that they submit other pieces of information, either to you directly or to the platform you are using. I typically require a picture of their driver's license and their most recent two pay stubs.

It's a lot to take in, but you must be as thorough as possible. Your rental income is dependent on qualified, responsible, rent-paying tenants.

## Property management

At this point, you might *still* be thinking, "But how is this passive?"

It's not passive... at first.

But the thing is, every single passive income stream I've mentioned requires an upfront time or capital investment or both. Stage 1 is not passive! It takes time to write a book, capital to generate portfolio income, time and money to open a laundromat, time to monetize a blog, and time and money to invest in a rental property.

The goal with any of these ideas is to streamline them over time, outsource them, or hire someone to manage them for you so that you don't have to work.

For rental income, that's where the property manager comes in. For the record, I think it's highly valuable at first to do this completely on your own. Learn, chart your own territory, create your own documents and systems. But the ultimate goal is to hire a property manager who can do it all for you. *That's* when it becomes *true* passive income.

*The ultimate goal is to hire a property manager who can do it all for you. That's when it becomes true*

**"**

Even without a property manager, managing rentals is way easier than a full-time job. Take our duplex, for example. We do year-long leases, are very strict about our requirements, and therefore have very clean, rent-paying tenants. Unless we are between tenants, we spend an average of one hour per month managing the property, and it now generates $800 in net cash flow.

But once you get to twenty, thirty, or fifty units, it's a different ball game. Now you're talking a part-time job or several hours per week, and you might not want that. The cost of hiring a property manager should be factored into the property financial analysis before you even buy—that way, you'll always have it as an option.

You have the option of hiring a property management company or an individual. A property management company will already know the ropes and will collect anywhere from 5% to 15% of rent revenue. That's rent *revenue,* not rent profit. They will also be licensed and insured, which covers you if anything goes wrong.

With an individual, you will either have to find someone who is properly licensed and can work for you as an independent contractor, or you'll have to employ them. Be careful because the rules differ by state. Hiring an individual gives you more flexibility in terms of what you would pay. Normally, a larger property management company sets its rate, and you can't really negotiate with them.

Hiring a trustworthy, reliable property manager is no easy feat, and I want to be transparent with you. I've been through hell trying to find a good property manager. It was super fun when earlier this year, my two "trusted" employees stole $6,000 of my rent money and disappeared. I learned a lot of lessons there: First, don't hire an individual off Craigslist as your property manager, even if they have proven themselves to be hard-working and dedicated and have worked with you for a long time in other areas of your life. Second, trust the credit and background check, not the person. Credit and background checks don't lie; people do. Third, go with a licensed and insured professional, like a real estate agent or property management company. I beg you: learn from my costly mistakes.

As you can see, in no way am I trying to make this out to be extremely easy, because those of you who are already landlords know that it's not. It might take a few tries before you land on the right person or company.

As you can also see, the bad times as a landlord have not dissuaded me from owning rental property. For me, when it comes to rental properties, nothing outweighs the benefits of passive income and the lucrative cash flow.

## The Magic

I prefer rental income over the other passive income streams because of the three huge benefits: you're generating passive cash flow, you're building equity and wealth over time, *and* you're getting a tax benefit.

I'm going to show you a fun scenario based on my original goal with rental property investing. The plan was to buy one single-family home every year for ten years, all on 15-year mortgages. This was the basis of my early retirement plan. I want to show you how this scenario could play out.

Let's say you buy just ONE single family property on a 15-year mortgage that generates $250 per month in net cash flow. For the next 15 years, you'll make $250 per month with minimal work. After 15 years is when the real magic begins because your mortgage is paid off. Suddenly, you own a home free and clear that you didn't even pay for! All you had to do was put 20% to 25% down (or less if you used one of the strategies in Chapter 20), and then you made $250 per month *while your tenant was paying your mortgage for you.*

Not only do you own an entire house outright after 15 years, but also your cash flow jumps by hundreds of dollars more since your mortgage payment goes away. From then on, you could be making $500, $800, or $1,200 per month on that same property.

Now get this. Let's say you buy one single-family property each year for ten years. In year one, you're making $250 per month. In year two, $500 per month. Year three, $750 per month. And so forth. By year ten, you own ten units, each generating $250 per month in net cash flow, or $2,500 total.

But the real magic happens in year sixteen when your first mortgage is paid off. Let's say that having the mortgage paid off frees up another $600 per month. Check it out. Here's what your cash flow situation would look like from year one through year twenty.

| | # of Properties Owned | Monthly cash flow | Annual cash flow |
|---|---|---|---|
| Year 1 | 1 | 250 | 3,000 |
| Year 2 | 2 | 500 | 6,000 |
| Year 3 | 3 | 750 | 9,000 |
| Year 4 | 4 | 1,000 | 12,000 |
| Year 5 | 5 | 1,250 | 15,000 |
| Year 6 | 6 | 1,500 | 18,000 |
| Year 7 | 7 | 1,750 | 21,000 |
| Year 8 | 8 | 2,000 | 24,000 |
| Year 9 | 9 | 2,250 | 27,000 |
| Year 10 | 10 | 2,500 | 30,000 |
| Year 11 | 10 | 2,500 | 30,000 |
| Year 12 | 10 | 2,500 | 30,000 |
| Year 13 | 10 | 2,500 | 30,000 |
| Year 14 | 10 | 2,500 | 30,000 |
| Year 15 | 10 | 2,500 | 30,000 |
| **Year 16** | **10** | **3,100** | **37,200** |
| Year 17 | 10 | 3,700 | 44,400 |
| Year 18 | 10 | 4,300 | 51,600 |
| Year 19 | 10 | 4,900 | 58,800 |
| Year 20 | 10 | 5,500 | 66,000 |

In year 15, the revenue is $30k; five years later, it's more than doubled at $66k. And the cash flow will keep increasing from there as you pay off another mortgage each year! In just a couple of decades, you'll have built an enormous income stream that will last you for the rest of your life. Starting this plan in your twenties means you can retire in your thirties or forties, given that you keep your cost of living in line.

Guys, this was *my* plan. Except that once I bought my first duplex, things really started accelerating for me. My duplex generated $500 per month, and I put that straight into savings. I wanted to reinvest in the rental business. Andrew and I bought our next property nine months later, and the next rental four months after that. Once you start making rental income, your savings can snowball rapidly. In under three years, I'm already generating $7,000+ per month *in rental income alone*. Because of my experience, I believe that the above chart is quite conservative.

It's pretty freaking fantastic that, with real estate, you can easily do in twenty years what most people fail to do by age 65. Not to mention all the equity you'll have by then—in the millions!

Real estate is THE number one wealth-building investment possible. Period.

## Conclusion

What a gold mine of information! In this chapter, we discussed all things rental income. We started by covering the difference between direct and indirect rental income, and we looked at a few non-traditional ideas, including AirBNBs, storage spaces, and even car ad space.

Then, we got into residential rental property investing and its three primary benefits: cash flow or passive income, equity build-up, and tax benefits. We considered cash vs. leveraging when it comes to buying property. We discussed all the different ways to fund your property, including house hacking and the BRRRR method.

We also thought about all the different ways to find deals (besides just the MLS.) We learned how to analyze the property using the three big metrics: cash flow, cash-on-cash ROI, and capitalization rate. We learned how to make an offer and find tenants and also about the importance of hiring a property manager. We even got to hear from two real estate moguls, David Osborn and Doug Skipworth!

And as you now know, I'm a big fan of rental property because it provides passive income and several other financial benefits. Even before I became an expert in all things passive income, I had identified rental properties as the best wealth-building tool. I believe every person should own a rental property.

This caps off our in-depth study of the five main categories of passive income! You now have all the information, knowledge, and know-how. So, what next? Where do you go from here? Let's put it all together and figure out how to get started!

# SECTION SEVEN:

# Now What?

# CHAPTER 23

## *The Fun Part*

Wow! Your brain is probably overloaded with technical and exciting information. Luckily, there are few feelings as energizing as unlocking the potential of financial freedom, flexibility, and stability. It's a welcome overwhelm, isn't it?

We started down this journey together by looking at how our world has changed over the past 70+ years. We studied and debunked the Nest Egg Theory, analyzed our most valuable resource (time!), and finally landed on passive income as the solution for achieving financial independence.

We discussed what passive income is and how it works. Passive income requires an upfront time or money investment to create. We call this Stage 1. Then you have Stage 2, which occurs after you've built the income stream. Stage 2 is where it really becomes passive, and you can chillax. You're finally bringing in money with little to no work.

Then we had an in-depth overview of the five main categories of passive income: Royalties, Portfolio Income, Coin-Operated Machines, Ads and E-commerce, and Rental Income. Not everything is 100% passive, but the ideas in *PIAR* all come close, and they are *all* low-maintenance compared to working a 9-5.

And we are now in the most exciting part of the book—where we puzzle together all the pieces, what this means for *you*, and how you can apply it! And we'll take all the stress out of the equation by figuring out together where you want to go and how to get there.

In this chapter, we are going to look at your goals (where you *want* to be) versus your current situation (where you *are*). Then, we will bridge the gap and figure out exactly how to get there.

There's a lot of action in the following chapters. You'll need to discipline yourself and complete each and every activity.

*he first step towards financial independence is getting your financial $hit together. You have to build the foundation before you . ..*

Now, let me give you a very serious caution. My first book, *Money Honey*, is about getting your financial $hit together. And that's the very first step towards financial independence. You have to build the foundation before you put the walls up. The foundation consists of basic money management: how to budget, save, pay off debt, invest, pay taxes, and insure. If you are lacking in these areas, that's where you *must* start.

Building passive income requires sound money management; you need to walk before you run. I would be remiss if I didn't tell you to get your financial $hit together first, and *then* work your way towards early retirement with passive income.

The strategy we review from here until the end of the book is made under the following assumptions:

1) You know that building passive income is hard work. There is no such thing as a get-rich-scheme. You are ready to dedicate and commit yourself to building passive income streams so that you can become truly financially independent.

2) Your finances are in order. You are proficient with the fundamentals, including budgeting, savings, debt payoff, and investing. Passive income is the natural next step.

3) You either have time (or you're willing to free up your time) or capital. If you need help with this, I'll elaborate on how to do this because it can be one of the biggest challenges.

## Today

Let's start by taking a look at your current situation.

How much are your current monthly expenses? You should know this number or be able to access it easily if you are tracking your spending. Your total monthly expenses are the amount of money you'd need to maintain your lifestyle for one month. Ideally, not only will you know your total expenses, but you'll also know how much you spend in each category (housing, transportation, food, and so forth.)

Go ahead and write this number down now. Put the book down for a hot sec to grab a pen and paper, get the Notes app out on your phone, or pull up a Word doc on your laptop.

Also, you'll want to understand how much debt you have and how much you have in savings. You can make note of these figures on the same piece of paper or Word doc. Go on, I'm not going anywhere!

## Designing Your Dream Life

Now for the good stuff! Our objective is to visualize what we really want in our life. Just to stimulate your brain juices, ponder the following questions, which were first brought up in Chapter 3:

- If money didn't exist, how would you spend your time?
- What would you do if you only had one year left to live?
- What would you do if you won $20 million in the lottery? What would you do at first, and what would you do later?

Additional questions include:

- What are you passionate about?
- What do you love to tell your family and friends about? What do you love to learn about?

You really need to think about what drew you to this book in the first place. Is it because you want to get out of that corporate 9-5 life? Do you hate your job? Fine, we'll get you outta there. But have you thought about what you'd want to do instead? Once those hours are freed up, how will you spend them? It's easy to think, "I hate my situation/job/life, leaving will make me happy." But what's the alternative? What will you do with your time instead? Maybe you'll travel the world. Maybe you'll start a nonprofit. Maybe you'll read a hundred books in a month or finally train to run a marathon. Whatever you decide is fine, just make sure you know. Don't be so focused on the *getting away* from something that you forget about the *going to* something else.

> on't be so focused on the **getting away** from something that you forget about the **going to** something else.

Are you reading *PIAR* because you want to have supplemental income to support your lifestyle? Perfect, we can do that. If you're sick of living paycheck to paycheck or always being stressed out about your finances, passive income is the solution. Money that comes in with minimal work can be a great way to minimize stress, free up time to spend with your kids, or simply free up your budget!

Maybe you love your lifestyle or your job, but you don't want to depend on work for your money... you want financial *independence*. You want the flexibility and freedom of being able to do whatever you want.

Did you pick up this book because you like a good rich-quick-scheme? Bzzzz, wrong answer! You should know this by now: creating a passive income stream takes work.

Maybe you want to raise your kids without having to leave for work for 45 hours a week. Or maybe you're a stay-at-home parent who feels drawn to do something in addition to the incredibly challenging responsibility of raising kids. Maybe you want to have a passion project on the side.

Whatever your reason behind creating passive income, know it, and write it down. Answer those questions now. Write out some ideas and thoughts in a bulleted list on your document.

Let your WHY motivate you and excite you. Let it sustain you through those difficult times when you're cursing this book and me because well $hit, building passive income is hard to create, and you might fail seven times before you finally succeed. Your WHY is the most essential ingredient to success.

## Getting from Here to There

You know your monthly expenses, you've envisioned your dream life, and you've defined your WHY. The next step is calculating how much passive income you'll need to live your ideal life.

Maybe the life you have now IS ideal. And that's fine. Actually, that makes it easy. Because if your lifestyle and spending stay the same, then the passive income you need is equal to your current monthly expenses. Done. This will be the case for many people reading *PIAR*.

If the life you envision is quite a bit different, we'll need to take that into account. For instance, maybe you're someone who really wants to quit your job and live your dream life. Let's say, in your ideal life, you move from Tennessee to the Oregon Coast. Let's also say you quit your job so you can spend more time traveling.

Just from those assumptions, I'm hearing many different things: You're moving from a LCOL area to an HCOL area. You're moving to a part of the country that has some of the highest housing costs. Quitting your job could mean you'll have to find health insurance elsewhere, and that could be pricey. Traveling can be expensive. It sounds like you'll need to increase your expenses significantly to fund this lifestyle.

Housing costs, health insurance, and childcare expenses are the three biggest items to consider. Do your research and know how much they will cost you ahead of time. Then, mark it up another 20% or 30% to be safe. It's better to be conservative and come in under your estimated expenses.

Think through all your spending categories. Will you be spending more in your ideal life on food or eating out? Will utilities cost more or less? What about entertainment? What about expenses for your children or pets? The easiest way to think through your spending is to outline your entire budget by category based on today's expenses, and then make another column showing your proposed expenses.

My husband and I did this exact activity before we ever started building passive income. Andrew and I lived a comfy lifestyle, and we didn't want to give that up in order to retire. In fact, I wanted to spend even more money in early retirement. Some categories that increased in our proposed expenses column were travel, health insurance, and housing.

> **"**
> *The great thing about passive income is that you don't **have** to reduce your*
> **"**

the opposite; maybe you want to give up ne luxuries to be able to retire earlier. ny in the FIRE community find ways to frugally, enabling them to retire on less ney. That's fine too, and if you go that ite, you'll likely be able to achieve your ls earlier than the rest of us who don't nt to cut back. But let me be clear: the great thing about passive income is that you don't *have* to reduce your quality of life.

Also, consider whether you want to continue to build up your savings. Some people may want more passive income instead of just enough to cover expenses. That way, they can continue to save money for big-ticket items like a wedding, down payment on a house, or a college education for their kids. This makes sense! You're in charge here. Think about how much per month you'd like to save and add it to your total proposed expenses. If your ideal lifestyle will cost $6,500, and you want to save $1,500 per month, then your passive income number is $8,000 per month.

Write these proposed expenses down now in your working document.

Now you know precisely what you are working towards. You have your WHY. You know what retirement means to you and what your ideal lifestyle looks like. You know how much monthly passive income you'll need to make it happen.

Your map is complete! The next step is determining the route—figuring out how to go from Point A to Point B. In the next chapter, we'll discuss how to pick the best passive income stream for *you*.

# CHAPTER 24

# Drumroll...Your first passive income stream

As I have said many-a-time, building a passive income stream takes work. This book isn't some scam on how to make a quick buck and retire next month.

Creating passive income requires one of two things: TIME or MONEY.

So, the first thing to consider is whether you have more time or money at your disposal. You'll absolutely need at least one to build your passive income streams.

If your immediate thought is, "Uh, neither!" then don't worry. I felt the same way when I first started. I was always trapped in my never-ending to-do list. How could I possibly free up time? And I don't even have kids! I don't know how you moms do it. #MadRespect.

*PIAR* isn't about time management, but I do have an important learning lesson to share. Once I took a good, hard look at my schedule, I noticed a couple of time-wasters. Actually, after tracking my time in 15-

minute intervals for two entire days (yes, I actually did this) and then categorizing how I was spending my time (hey! I just realized I essentially did a BUDGET for my TIME), it was embarrassingly apparent where approximately three hours of my time was going every day: social media and TV *Cringe.* The funny thing is, I always talked about how little time

> *Creating passive income requires one of two things: TIME or MONEY.* "

I had, complained about how stressed I was, and turned down social events because I couldn't squeeze them into my schedule. But it wasn't until I actually sat down and tracked where my time was going that I saw all the ways I wasted it. I felt like a hypocrite!

Figuring out how your time is spent is exactly like doing a financial budget. Sometimes you don't see the obvious until you track it. So, let's not guess or pretend like we know how we spend our time. Let's be really clear and do this tracking exercise for two days. Included in the *PIAR* Bonus Gift is the tracking template I used to do just this, so make sure to download it at **www.moneyhoneyrachel.com/bonus**—it's totally free!

I know, I know, not all of you are gluttonous social media addicts like I am, and you may not easily free up three hours per day just like that. This exercise won't necessarily be that easy. But still, DO the exercise, and take a good hard look at what you spend your time on.

Are you waiting for 15 minutes in the carpool line for your kids each day? Great! Bring a notebook with you and brainstorm your passive income ideas. Have you ever had a doctor's appointment and sat in the waiting room for 35 minutes? That's another opportunity to be productive. In fact, always bring a book, notebook, or laptop with you when you leave the house! Is there a more efficient way you could be prepping food, such as doing it all at once, instead of making a meal every night? Same with laundry—can you "time block" laundry or any other chores?

I sacrificed a lot to free up time. (I mean, giving up social media and TV is hardly a sacrifice.) But also, I temporarily didn't go out with my friends or family as much, opting instead to work more on my passive income streams. Before I hired house cleaners, I decided to clean every other week instead of every week and just accept the mountains of Chloe's fur piling up in every corner. Am I saying you should do these things? No. I'm not here to tell you what to do or not to do. Am I saying building passive income requires sacrifice? Yes. It will take effort. You will probably have to give something up in the short term to pursue this. One way or another, you will have to find a way to free up more time.

On the other side of the coin (pun intended), maybe you have available capital, or you can easily save up capital.

Let me remind you of the only two ways to save more money:

1)  Spend less money

2)  Make more money

That's it. All you can do is decrease your expenses or increase your income. Again, if you have room in your budget to cut back (you'll only know if you actually track your expenses), then do so. You'll need to make sacrifices here too. Can you give up cable? Netflix, Hulu, Amazon Prime? Can you completely stop eating out for two months? Can you be better about buying things when they're on sale at the grocery store? Can you do simple things like turning off lights and unplugging things when you're not home? What can you give up temporarily so that you can save more money?

You can also increase your earned income, which can ironically turn into a Catch-22 that we want to avoid. So be careful: I'm not advising you to spend more time working. But you could consider asking for a raise or going for a promotion at work. Think about looking for a higher-paying job. Are there other ways to increase your earned income without increasing your time spent working?

Ask yourself: do you have more time, or do you have more money? If you have neither right now, that's okay. Which one is going to be easier for you to free up?

## Narrowing Your Options

As you work on freeing up your time or money, you can decide on which passive income stream to pursue first. Let's take a look at all the different passive income streams we have discussed. Here's an easy outline to which you can refer.

Royalties (requires mostly time; minimal or no money)

- Books, eBooks, audio books
- Music
- Photography
- Downloadable content
- PODs
- Online courses
- Software or app development
- Franchising
- Mineral Rights

Portfolio Income (requires no time; lots of money)

- Dividend income
- Bond income
- Interest income
- P2P
- MLPs
- REITs
- Crowdfunded real estate

Coin-Operated Machines (requires some time and some money)

- Vending machines
- ATM vendor
- Arcade games
- Car wash
- Laundromat
- Slot machines

Advertising and E-commerce (requires mostly time; minimal money)

- Affiliate marketing

- Advertising
- Dropshipping

Rental Income (requires some time and some money)
- Airbnb or VRBO
- Storage space
- Residential real estate

That's 28 ideas! Some will automatically jump out at you, and others you may have already crossed off in your mind. Feel free to mark on this page and cross any off that you know you don't want to pursue, or that you can't pursue because of the time or money requirement. For example, if you don't have money available for an upfront capital investment and no means of getting that money, you might cross off the portfolio income section altogether. That's exactly what I did. If you don't have time or interest in building up a platform or following, you might cross off affiliate marketing or advertising. It's a long list, so don't be afraid to cross off lots of options! We are trying to narrow it down, after all.

In addition, put a star next to any ideas that excite you or for which you already have a skillset.

The goal here is to narrow your options down to the best three or four that will work within your constraints. You don't need experience, skills, or even passion for any of them. Passive income isn't about doing what you love. It's about building up income streams so that you can THEN do what you love. Be practical and identify three or four solid options.

## Using the Factors of SCRIMP

From here, the final step is to review the Factors of SCRIMP so that you can land on the best passive income stream out of those three or four options.

Again, here are the Factors of SCRIMP:

1) Scalability: Can it be produced or offered en masse?
2) Controllability & Regulation: How much control do you have over it?

3) Investment: How much time or money will you need to invest during Stage 1?

4) Marketability: Is there a need for it?

5) Passivity: How much work is it to maintain in Stage 2?

Determine which factors are the most important to you. Some readers might want something that is 100% passive or as close to completely passive as possible. Some readers want to be able to scale their passive income streams easily. Some readers want full control and minimal regulation over their passive income.

Reorganize the Factors of SCRIMP from one to five based on your priorities. Finally, using the order of priority and your three or four passive income stream options, you can decide on which is THE best passive income stream to pursue *first*. You don't have to limit yourself to just one; try your top pick *first*. Once you have that going, look back at your options and implement your second pick.

An unlimited amount of potential passive income streams coupled with the five Factors of SCRIMP could result in decision paralysis—you know, the complete lack of ability to decide. If you're feeling this way at all, I highly recommend using a weighted decision matrix. This ingenious decision matrix takes all the guessing out of the equation. You can look online to see how they work and create one for yourself.

# CHAPTER 25

# Limiting Beliefs Are for the Birds

Everything in this book is all well and good, but it's entirely meaningless unless you *take action*. And that's the hardest part. It's hard because, first of all, we all naturally resist change and tend to default into what's normal. Starting a new diet or workout plan is hard because it requires effort. Starting a new job is hard because it's scary. You might fail. The techniques in *PIAR* aren't fail-proof. Anyone can try them; not everyone will be successful. And that's a scary thought. What if you put your money into something that doesn't work out? What if you invest your time into something that doesn't make any money?

We all have limiting beliefs.

My dear uncle once bet me $200 that I could not complete the Grand Canyon rim-to-rim hike. That was his roundabout way of trying to motivate me to prove him wrong. The problem was that I was already discouraged and disappointed with myself because I hadn't been working out, and I'd witnessed my sisters outperform me athletically for my whole life. Once my uncle made that bet with me, I agreed with him. I couldn't escape from that negative feedback loop.

My limiting belief? I was not an athlete. That belief stayed with me for *four* years, until I got in the best shape of my life and completed that hike not once, but TWICE.

Other limiting beliefs might be:

*I'm not good enough.*

*I have no willpower.*

*I don't deserve this promotion.*

*It's too late for me to change.*

*I'm too old for X, Y, Z.*

These beliefs hold us back, and by believing them, we constrain ourselves. It's a self-fulfilling prophecy.

If you are feeling the (very normal) fear of pursuing one of these passive income streams, ask yourself what your limiting belief is. That's where the fear is rooted. Is it that you don't think you can do it? That you don't deserve to invest time into this because family comes first?

Is it simply the "What if?" What if I fail? What if I lose my money? What if I lose my significant other's money? Any business venture involves risk. Luckily, a lot of these passive income streams require time instead of money. But still... what if you lose or waste your time? What if it's all for nothing?

> *The techniques in PIAR aren't fail-proof. Anyone can try them; not everyone will be successful. And that's a scary thought.*

Here are some of the most common limiting beliefs when it comes to passive income:

I don't have time, or I don't have money: please refer back to Chapter 24 on how to free up time and/or money.

I'm not good at selling or marketing. You don't have to be good at anything right now. You *do* have to be willing to learn and willing to try. I never took a single course in marketing before I published *Money*

*Honey*. I followed the launch plan in Chandler Bolt's book *Published*, and that was successful for me. And to be honest, I'm not great at marketing my POD design business. It's fallen to the wayside. I used to be better on social media, but there's a ton more I could be doing. *You don't have to know how to do any of this*. You can begin researching and teaching yourself, or you can learn as you go, which is largely what I have done. If one marketing technique doesn't work, move onto the next. Be willing to tweak things until you get it right. Get a mentor. Work with a professional. Get some coaching or some help. There're a billion things you can do to learn and get better; being good at marketing is not a prerequisite for building passive income.

I'm scared to risk losing my money. I'm scared too. Wanna know what I'm *more* afraid of? Being dependent on a job for a paycheck. Because guess what? I could lose my job, too. And then what do I do? I'd much rather have an independent income stream to support me rather than being dependent on a paycheck.

If you're scared of investing your money into a passive income stream, determine exactly how much would be so much that you'd never forgive yourself for losing it. For me, I wasn't willing to invest a ton of money into *Money Honey* because, to be honest, I was super scared and vulnerable and unsure of myself. I capped it at $600. I could have spent even less. I was okay with losing $600 to try out this whole self-publishing thing. And guess what? I made $600 just in the first month after I launched *Money Honey*.

Maybe you are willing to risk more or less. Many of the passive income streams don't require money anyway; if money is your worry, then focus on those instead. I was much more willing to invest in a rental because I knew the numbers going in. I KNEW it would generate revenue; it wasn't up to my marketing abilities to generate income. You won't gain anything if you don't put yourself out there, but there's also no reason to risk losing your money at all. You can focus on one of the options that only require an investment of time.

I don't have any ideas. I used to feel the exact same way. I had to change my entire way of thinking. I began forcing myself to observe and question other businesses. If I went to get ice cream, I'd wonder how many orders they have per day, how much it cost them, and how much they profited. I began thinking like an entrepreneur. I am constantly aware if I get annoyed with a particular product or service (or lack thereof). Sometimes I'll think,

"It would be so much easier if I had something that could do THIS!" Wait... what if I created that something? What if I filled the market need? Try to be more observant of the world around you. What are your coworkers frustrated with? What do your family and friends wish they knew more about? Is there a passive income stream idea there? Carry around a notebook and begin brainstorming and writing down notes, observations, and ideas and see where it gets you after a couple of weeks.

I don't have enough skills. Besides marketing, which we addressed above, some of the skills you might *think* you need are: writing, photography, creating music, learning how to record audio or video on your device, prospecting, cold calling, researching, designing, managing, or something else. You do not need these skills right now. A lot of this you can learn as you go. Do I recommend trying to sell stock photos if you've never been interested in or good at photography? No. Play to your strengths, but please don't *you go. But you must get started.* certain skills to do this. If you have an awesome book idea but suck at writing, get a ghostwriter. If you want to create a downloadable template, look up some Photoshop tutorials. See if it's something you can teach yourself. Or work with a pro; hire an Upwork freelancer who can put your vision into reality. You don't necessarily need to do this yourself. Anything can be learned or hired out.

You'll learn a ton as you go, and you'll make mistakes along the way, just as I have with every single passive income stream I've built. But you must get started. Just start somewhere. Read one article; reach out to one contact; call one apartment complex to ask about their laundry situation. Don't let this limiting belief stop you.

I'm scared of the stock market. *PIAR* is about passive income, and it's not a guide about investing in the stock market. Wouldn't it be nice if I wrote something about that? Oh, wait, I did! In *Money Honey*, I have a full section describing what the different types of investments are and how to buy and sell stocks with screenshots and everything. It's one of the most valuable sections of my first book. Of course, I'm biased. You can also find hundreds of resources online. Investing in the stock market is a lot simpler than most people think. Grab a book or do some research online to start getting familiar with the terms. Know what a stock or bond is. Understand a mutual fund and index fund. The more familiar you are, the less scared you will be. I promise it's easier than you think!

I just can't do all these. Not everybody can succeed at all of these passive income ideas! But can you succeed at *one*? Because one is all it takes. Trust me, most of these passive income streams are out of my league. People would pay *not* to listen to a song I've written. No one is going to buy a cookbook I write, not even my mother. I could look at my list and cross off 75% of the options easily. You and I are different people. What works for you might not work for me, and that's okay! There's an op You know what's available. Just pick *one*. You can do this.

> one*? Because one is all it takes.* **"**

If some other limiting belief is holding you back, write it down in your journal. And then write down what you think my response would be. Or what your friend's response would be if you confided in her. Or write down how you would respond to your friend if she told you about this particular limiting belief. Figure out why it's holding you back and how you can overcome it. Determine if it's worth overcoming. Is your WHY strong enough?

Limiting beliefs are for the birds. They're legitimate, founded fears, but they're for the birds. You don't need that kind of negativity in your life!

Don't let fear hold you back from pursuing this. Define how much risk you are willing to take on. Take it one day at a time. You can only overcome your limiting beliefs if you know what they are in the first place.

Building a passive income stream can be hard work, but you can definitely do it. Think back to your WHY and let that motivate you.

## What if you succeed?

If you're stuck in that cycle of fear (and believe me, that's *exactly* how I felt in the middle of writing *Money Honey*), I challenge you to consider this: What if you just forget about all this? What if you stay in your job? What if you don't do anything differently? What if you never experience financial independence? How do you feel thinking about trudging into work every single weekday for the next 10, 20, 30, or 40 years of your life? What if you never get to see the world and do all you dream of because you never have the time or money?

BUT...

What if you succeed?

What if you make a lot of money?

What if the time invested was well worth it?

What if you slowly but surely get passive income streams into place?

And what if, one day, you're not dependent on your job for money?

What if you gain flexibility and freedom from your passive income?

## A Couple Last Thoughts

Don't get ahead of yourself. Don't make any crazy changes in your lifestyle just because you're starting to pursue passive income. Alisha Ramos, the founder of *Girls Night In*, once said, "'Just quit your job and do it' is bad and privileged advice." She is 100% right. You can't afford to quit your job UNTIL you've replaced your income! So, be patient. Passive income will get you to retirement a lot sooner than you would otherwise, but it still takes hard work to make it happen.

> *do it' is bad and privileged advice.*
> Alisha Ramos

Don't miss out on the supplemental resources in your free *PIAR* Bonus Gift! You can download it now at: **www.moneyhoneyrachel.com/bonus**.

Speak to your CPA or do your research on any financial, legal, or tax implications before getting started. In official IRS tax speak, passive income and portfolio income are two different things and are taxed differently. You should understand how they are taxed and how said taxes would impact you. You should understand that passive income losses cannot be offset by portfolio or active income. Your responsibility is to be fully informed first and foremost; after all, I'm no tax expert!

## Conclusion

And here we are... only a few pages left, lots of ideas, some nerves and excitement, and most importantly... hope.

My goal with this book is to give you hope.

We've all become so discouraged. We have student loans and debt payments and bills to pay, and we don't make enough money. How will we ever reach retirement at age 65, let alone retire early? Yes, some high earners can live extremely frugally and save a ton in a short span of time to buy their freedom, but what about the rest of us?

The answer is that financial independence is accessible to *everyone* via passive income. Once your passive income exceeds your monthly living expenses, you are *retired*. You are *financially independent*. You are finally free to go wherever you want to go and do whatever you want to do. Money will not constrain you anymore.

Passive income is your golden ticket... your chance to finally live a life of complete financial freedom.

## Go... Go Now

If you commit yourself, do your research, have a thorough business plan, know what to expect, and have that valuable trait called *tenacity*, I have no doubt you will succeed. You absolutely can make this happen.

In just two short years, my husband and I went from zero passive income to $10,000+ per month and are well on our way to a much higher number. If you asked me two years ago if I thought that was possible, I would have said, "You're crazy!" I mean, I graduated college broke and started out making $32,000 per year. I had no *clue* then that I'd be here today, retired at age 27. I didn't plan for it all to happen the way it did, but we worked our butts off, we were very fortunate in many ways, and we had great opportunities.

> *I can do it, so can you. I am no better or more impressive or more capable than anyone reading this book. I just worked hard.* "

If I can do it, so can you. I am no better or more impressive or more capable than anyone reading this book. I just worked *hard*. I did the work to make it happen, and now I'm here. I was in the same boat as you a mere two years ago. Until I decided I wanted *options*.

In the near future, you could have generated $1,000, $2,000, or $5,000 a month in passive income. You could even be fully retired. You could make that ideal lifestyle that you wrote about in Chapter 23 a reality. What would you do if you no longer had to work? Instead of wondering and dreaming, you could actually know and be living this life in a couple of years.

You could be sitting at a cafe in Florence, Italy, simply because you were in the mood for authentic ribollita. You could hop over to Paris the next week. You could fly home to visit your family and friends for extended periods of time. You could work on knocking out your bucket list. You could finally do that thing you've always wanted to do but kept putting off. You could volunteer your time and give back to the community in meaningful ways. You could be a financially self-sufficient stay-at-home parent without having to go to work. You could sit on your couch and cuddle your kids with no money stressors on your mind. You could dedicate your time to raising your kids. You could start a nonprofit daycare for parents who can't afford daycare. You could find a cause to rally around. You could become involved in politics and fight for what you believe in. You could explore any and every option—because you would have the time and financial freedom to do so.

I'll leave you with this. There's so much exciting opportunity in this world, and we have such a short time here. How do you want to spend it? How would flexibility, freedom, and financial independence change your life?

# ACKNOWLEDGMENTS

I'd like to thank the people who were most impacted by my round-the-clock obsession with perfecting this book in the month leading up to my launch:

My husband, Andrew, is a Godsend. He grocery shopped, cooked my meals, and took care of business so that I did not completely lose my mind. He is as responsible for the successful release of *Passive Income, Aggressive Retirement* as I am. How did I get so lucky?

To the Poopfaces: Mom, Dad, Lauren, and Claire. Y'all are the $hit.

To my fur baby, Chloe: Thanks for periodically resting your head on my laptop to remind me to take breaks.

To my launch team of over 500 people: All I can think about is how many polls you suffered through so that I could get pick out a title, LOL. You guys put up with a lot and I'm so touched by your continued support. Internet friends are the best.

I'd also like to thank my readers. My Money Honies are the most enthusiastic, supportive, and kind people I know. Your passion for learning gets me fired up. And to my newest readers, thank you for taking a chance on me and reading *PIAR*. May the odds be ever in your favor!

I've been working with the greatest editor of all time, Kate Johnson, since the birth of *Money Honey*. Kate, your edits have given me confidence in my writing. Thank you for honing my craft with your wizardry.

# RECOMMENDED READING

*Money Honey: A Simple 7-Step Guide for Getting Your Financial $hit Together* by Yours Truly

*Published* by Chandler Bolt

*The Miracle Morning* by Hal Elrod

*The Miracle Equation* by Hal Elrod

*Miracle Morning Millionaires* by Hal Elrod, David Osborn, and Honorée Corder

*Wealth Can't Wait* by David Osborn

*You Must Write a Book* by Honorée Corder

*The Millionaire Fastlane* by MJ DeMarco

*Hold* by Steve Chader, Jennice Doty, Jim McKissack, and Linda McKissack

# URGENT PLEA!

## What Did You Think of *Passive Income, Aggressive Retirement*?

First of all, reader and friend, it was super nice of you to take a chance and purchase this book. You could have picked any book, and you picked mine! High-five.

If you enjoyed *PIAR* and found some benefit in reading this, I'd love to hear from you. I hope you can take two quick minutes to **post a review on Amazon**. Reviews are hard to come by, and my business relies on them. I would deeply appreciate it!

You can hop on Amazon and Goodreads to review *Passive Income, Aggressive Retirement* now.

Cheers!

-Rachel

# ABOUT THE AUTHOR

Only 27 years old, former financial advisor Rachel Richards has made a name for herself in the personal finance realm. She is the Amazon bestselling author of *Money Honey: A Simple 7-Step Guide for Getting Your Financial $hit Together*. She has been featured on the Penny Hoarder and the New York Times and has been contracted to speak at colleges. Rachel is also a real estate investor with 35 rental units. Her valuable money lessons have helped thousands of millennials work their way out of financial despair. She has successfully done what no one has done before: made the topic of money management fun, entertaining, and simple. Rachel is based in Louisville, KY, with her husband and dog.

Important tidbits from Rachel herself:
*"One time, I left the stove on overnight at my house. Once, when I saw my French professor on campus I accidentally said 'Hola' to him. The other day, I almost ate a raw burger because I thought it was cooked. I have my financial $hit together, but I definitely don't have my $hit together. Just keepin' it real!"*

Rachel would love to hear from you on social media!
Facebook: www.facebook.com/moneyhoneyrachel
Instagram: www.instagram.com/moneyhoneyrachel
Twitter: www.twitter.com/moneyhoneyrach

# DISCLAIMER & IMPORTANT INFORMATION

This book and its contents are for your personal use only and are protected by applicable copyright, patent, and trademark laws.

The information provided in this book is for general informational purposes only. It is not intended and under no circumstances should be construed as providing personal investment, tax, or legal advice or recommendations. The book also should not be construed as an offer to sell or the solicitation of an offer to buy, nor as a recommendation to buy, hold, or sell any security.

The author is not a registered investment advisor, a registered securities broker-dealer, or a certified financial planner, or otherwise licensed to give investment advice. All opinions, analyses, and information included herein are based on sources believed to be reliable, and the book has been written in good faith, but no representation or warranty of any kind, expressed or implied, is made, including but not limited to any representation or warranty concerning accuracy, completeness, correctness, timeliness, or appropriateness.

You are responsible for your own investment decisions, and each investor is solely responsible for analyzing and evaluating any information used or relied upon in making an investment decision. Before making any investment decision, you should thoroughly investigate the proposed investment, consider your personal situation, and consult with a qualified investment advisor. The information and opinions provided in this book should not be relied upon or used as a substitute for consultation with professional advisors.

The use of or reliance on the contents of this book is done solely at your own risk. No representation or warranty, expressed or implied, is made as to the accuracy, completeness, or correctness of this book's opinions, analyses, or information. Investment markets have inherent risks, there can be no guarantee of profits, and investors may lose money any time they invest in the stock market. Different types of investments involve varying degrees of risk, and there can be no assurance that any specific investment or strategy will be either suitable or profitable for a specific investment portfolio.

Past performance does not assure future returns. Therefore, no reader should assume that the performance of any investment approach discussed in this book will be profitable in the future, equal its past performance, or reach any performance objectives. The author shall have and accepts no liability of whatever nature in respect of any claims, damages, loss, or expense arising from or in connection with an investor's reliance on or use of this book.

In no event shall any reference to any third party or third-party product or service be construed as an approval or endorsement by the author. In particular, the author does not endorse or recommend the services of any particular broker, dealer, mutual fund company, or information provider.

The author may now or in the future have positions in or trade the securities discussed in the book.

247

# ENDNOTES

1 Craig S. New York Times corrects the misquote of Thoreau's 'quiet desperation' line. Poynter website. https://www.poynter.org/reporting-editing/2012/new-york-times-corrects-misquote-of-thoreaus-quiet-desperation-line/. April 30, 2012. Accessed October 21, 2019.

2 Kathleen E. 1 in 3 Americans have less than $5,000 saved for retirement—here's why so many people can't save. CNBC website. https://www.cnbc.com/2018/08/27/1-in-3-americans-have-less-than-5000-dollars-saved-for-retirement.html. August 27, 2018. Accessed October 21, 2019.

3 Megan L. Here's how much money Americans have saved at every age. CNBC website. https://www.cnbc.com/2018/08/28/how-much-money-americans-have-saved-at-every-age.html. August 28, 2018. Accessed October 21, 2019.

4 IRS guidelines would classify this as portfolio income, but by the definitions of this book outlined in Chapter 4, I categorize it as passive income.

5 Shaking my head

6 Jason L. The Righteous Small House: Challenging House Size and the Irresponsible American Dream. https://www.yesmagazine.org/planet/the-righteous-small-house-challenging-house-size-and-the-irresponsible-american-dream. January 29, 2010. Accessed October 21, 2019.

7 Robert D. Single-Family Home Size Increases at the Start of 2018. NAHB website. http://eyeonhousing.org/2018/05/single-family-home-size-increases-at-the-start-of-2018/. May 21, 2018. Accessed October 21, 2019.

8 Erin D. Average number of people per household in the United States from 1960 to 2018. Statista website. https://www.statista.com/statistics/183648/average-size-of-households-in-the-us/. Edited April 29, 2019. Accessed October 21, 2019.

9 Eliza B. Life Before Equal Pay Day: Portrait of a Working Mother in the 1950s. Time website. https://time.com/3759822/working-mother/. April 13, 2015. Accessed November 2, 2019.

10 The American Family Today. Pew Research Center website. https://www.pewsocialtrends.org/2015/12/17/1-the-american-family-today/. December 17, 2015. Accessed November 2, 2015.

11 Elizabeth A. United States Life Tables, 2003. National Vital Statistics Reports. https://www.cdc.gov/nchs/data/nvsr/nvsr54/nvsr54_14.pdf. Revised March 28, 2007. Accessed October 21, 2019.

12 Adele H., Miranda D., Lillian M. New Realities of an Older America. Stanford Center on Longevity. http://longevity3.stanford.edu/wp-content/uploads/2013/01/New-Realities-of-an-Older-America.pdf. 2010. Accessed October 21, 2019.

13 Retirement Changes Dramatically Over the Years. Senior Living website. https://www.seniorliving.org/library/retirement-changes-dramatically-over-years/. Accessed October 21, 2019.

[14] Patrica M., David A. Social Security: A Program and Policy History. Social Security Administration Website. https://www.ssa.gov/policy/docs/ssb/v66n1/v66n1p1.html. 2005. Accessed October 21, 2019.

[15] Social Security wage base increases to $128,700 for 2018. Thompson Reuters website. https://tax.thomsonreuters.com/news/social-security-wage-base-increases-to-128700-for-2018/. October 16, 2017. Accessed October 21, 2019.

[16] Ratio of Covered Workers to Beneficiaries. Social Security Administration website. https://www.ssa.gov/history/ratios.html. Accessed October 21, 2019.

[17] A Summary of the 2019 Annual Reports. Social Security Administration website. https://www.ssa.gov/oact/trsum/. Accessed October 21, 2019.

[18] $hit Outta Luck

[19] Camilo M. Price of College Increasing Almost 8 Times Faster Than Wages. Forbes website. https://www.forbes.com/sites/camilomaldonado/2018/07/24/price-of-college-increasing-almost-8-times-faster-than-wages/#72bbae8666c1. July 24, 2018. Accessed October 21, 2019.

[20] Trends in College Pricing Highlights. CollegeBoard website. https://research.collegeboard.org/trends/college-pricing/highlights. Accessed October 21, 2019.

[21] Erik O. Where Did the 40-Hour Workweek Come From? NBC News Website. https://www.nbcnews.com/news/us-news/where-did-40-hour-workweek-come-n192276. September 1, 2014. Accessed October 21, 2019.

[22] Lydia S. The "40-Hour" Workweek Is Actually Longer—by 7 Hours. Gallup Website. https://news.gallup.com/poll/175286/hour-workweek-actually-longer-seven-hours.aspx. August 29, 2014. Accessed October 21, 2019.

[23] Theresa A. Is it Time to Kill the 40-Hour Workweek? SHRM website. https://www.shrm.org/hr-today/news/hr-magazine/0217/pages/is-it-time-to-kill-the-40-hour-workweek.aspx. January 23, 2017. Accessed October 21, 2019.

[24] The Deloitte Global Millennial Survey 2019. Deloitte website. https://www2.deloitte.com/global/en/pages/about-deloitte/articles/millennialsurvey.html. Accessed October 21, 2019.

[25] Robert P. Millennials' new retirement number? $1.8 million (or more!) USA Today website. https://www.usatoday.com/story/money/columnist/powell/2016/03/29/millennials-new-retirement-number-18-million-more/81329246/. March 29, 2016. Accessed October 21, 2019.

[26] An Open Letter to Millennials on Retirement. Farm Bureau Financial Services website. https://www.fbfs.com/learning-center/an-open-letter-to-millennials-on-retirement. January 1, 2019. Accessed October 21, 2019.

[27] John R. Here's How Much a Millennial Needs to Save Each Month to Retire With $5 Million. Entrepeneur.com. https://www.entrepreneur.com/article/283524. October 11, 2016. Accessed October 21, 2019.

28 Monique M. The State of American Retirement: How 401(k)s have failed most American workers. Economic Policy Institute website. https://www.epi.org/publication/retirement-in-america/#charts. March 3, 2016. Accessed October 21, 2019.

29 Catherine C. Retirement Throughout the Ages: Expectations and Preparations of American workers. Transamerica Center website. https://www.transamericacenter.org/docs/default-source/resources/center-research/16th-annual/tcrs2015_sr_retirement_throughout_the_ages.pdf. May 2015. Accessed October 21, 2019.

30 Amelia J. Average Retirement Savings: Are You Normal? SmartAsset website. https://smartasset.com/retirement/average-retirement-savings-are-you-normal. April 16, 2019. Accessed October 21, 2019.

31 Hal H., Cassie M., Uri B. People Who Choose Time Over Money Are Happier. SAGE journals website. https://journals.sagepub.com/doi/abs/10.1177/1948550616649239. May 25, 2016. Accessed October 21, 2019.

32 Hal H., Cassie H. What Should You Choose: Time or Money? New York Times website. https://www.nytimes.com/2016/09/11/opinion/sunday/what-should-you-choose-time-or-money.html. September 9, 2016. Accessed October 21, 2019.

33 Joe P. Alabama Woman Stuck in NYC Traffic in 1902 Invented the Windshield Wiper. NPR website. https://www.npr.org/2017/07/25/536835744/alabama-woman-stuck-in-nyc-traffic-in-1902-invented-the-windshield-wiper. July 25, 2017. Accessed October 21, 2019.

34 Len M. How much should you charge for your online course? Podia.com. https://www.podia.com/articles/how-much-should-you-charge-for-your-online-course. Accessed October 21, 2019.

35 As of October 19, 2019.

36 Georgia M. What Percentage of Small Businesses Fail? (And Other Need-to-Know Stats). Fundera website. https://www.fundera.com/blog/what-percentage-of-small-businesses-fail. Updated September 10, 2019. Accessed October 21, 2019.

37 Ryan H. Can I make money by placing vending machines? Quora website. https://www.quora.com/Can-I-make-money-by-placing-vending-machines. January 26, 2015. Accessed October 21, 2019.

38 Understanding Dropshipping. Shopify.com https://www.shopify.com/guides/dropshipping/understanding-dropshipping. Accessed October 21, 2019.

39 Dan R. The Inside Track to Drop Shipping and Passive Income. YFS Magazine website. https://yfsmagazine.com/2017/06/16/the-inside-track-to-drop-shipping-and-passive-income/. June 16, 2017. Accessed October 21, 2019.

40 You can learn more about Roofstock at https://www.roofstock.com/one/learn/how-it-works

41 The "investor loan program" that Doug references is explained in more detail in this article: https://themortgagereports.com/40119/rentals-financing-and-managing-more-than-4-properties

CPSIA information can be obtained
at www.ICGtesting.com
Printed in the USA
BVHW071738080720
583177BV00001B/17/J

9 781087 849096